# I HAPPENED UPON A MIRACLE

# I HAPPENED UPON A MIRACLE

## Voices from the Gospels

### C. David McKirachan

*Illustrations by Simon Carr*

Westminster John Knox Press
Louisville, Kentucky

Scripture quotations from the New Revised Standard Version of the Bible are copyright © 1989 by the Division of Christian Education of the National Council of the Churches of Christ in the U.S.A. and are used by permission.

*Book design by Sharon Adams*
*Cover design by Terry Dugan Design*
*Cover illustration by Simon Carr*

First edition
Published by Westminster John Knox Press
Louisville, Kentucky

This book is printed on acid-free paper that meets the American National Standards Institute Z39.48 standard. ∞

PRINTED IN THE UNITED STATES OF AMERICA

01 02 03 04 05 06 07 08 09 00 — 10 9 8 7 6 5 4 3 2 1

**Library of Congress Cataloging-in-Publication Data**

A catalog record for this book is available from the Library of Congress.

ISBN 0-664-22341-9

*This book is dedicated to*
*J. Charles McKirachan and Caroline Eckel McKirachan.*
*Their love for each other and for me*
*formed my eyes and the world I see.*
*I hope they know.*

# Contents

# Foreword

*T*his book didn't begin as a book. It began as a frustration. I'm a preacher and I have the unenviable task of trying to communicate some of the meaning and magic of Christmas during a service of worship on Christmas Eve. It is not the best time to attempt the sharing of profound truths. People are high on the holiday or on eggnog. They are in church because it is what you do on Christmas Eve. So, in frustration, I decided I'd sneak up on them during worship, while they weren't expecting it. I thought I'd tell them the story. It's a great story. Besides, I realized the protagonists in the Gospel were just as preoccupied with their lives as the Christmas Eve Christians. But something touched those preoccupied folks that was so powerful, it still resonates and sings. So I let them speak. My prey in the pew were slightly dazed. It seemed to hit some nerve. It is now a tradition for me to tell a story at the late service. "Who ya going to be this year?" To tell the truth, I enjoy the drama.

In the process of letting these people from the Christmas story speak, I realized there were others, part of the larger story, who also had stories to tell, and so I let them. The individuals who encountered Jesus were full of passions and conflicts, of neuroses and strengths that we can understand, because we share them. Their very human reactions to this person we hold so high are accessible in ways that the mystery of the motives of God are not. Yet we often neglect these accessible, human folk in our consideration of the deep truths we embrace and with which we wrestle. But our theology is based on these human interactions that provided the context for God's action. These were the people who were touched by the center of our most profound contemplation. They cannot be neglected if we are to come to grips with how we are being touched by God.

My experience has been that these stories are a beginning. They act as a hook that grabs people's attention, allowing them to focus on the scripture's meaning and power. I have given each character an issue, a personal angle that not only provides a context for storytelling but grounds the scripture in the specific, as people's interactions with Jesus were grounded in the specific. It allows the scripture to become personal and hopefully more powerful. So the stories become a teaching tool as well as a resource for worship. I have used them for both.

But more than that, they are fun—a quality we sometimes overlook in our search for meaning. Perhaps we do this because our culture is so inundated with entertainment; we shun cheap lures that dilute the message. But though we must be careful not to water down the truth, are we not constrained to allow it to speak to the generation in which we live? Again we are brought back to the human context, to the human issues and interests that demand our attention. That is where scripture has its power. That is the driving force behind these stories.

My father said that the job of the pastor is to comfort the afflicted and to afflict the comfortable. May these stories comfort and afflict you in all the best ways.

I could not have written this book without the help of many people, too many to be mentioned, but some must be. My wife, Robin, told me I could, repeatedly. My sons, Jonathan and Benjamin, ooohed and aaahed at all the right moments. My sisters, Susie and Margaret, asked how it was going, even when it wasn't. Jane Waterhouse, storyteller and novelist, offered me the authority of an able writer and drove the project onward with friendship. Judy Northridge made the manuscript legible and orderly, a real feat in my vicinity. My editor, Nick Street, believed in it enough to be honest and helpful. Johnsonburg Camp and its staff gave me a place to retreat and write. And the members and friends of the Rockaway and Shrewsbury Churches listened and appreciated.

I want to thank Simon Carr for his insight and humility and artistic vision. He's a gas to work with.

*Then an angel of the Lord stood before them, and the glory of the Lord shone around them, and they were terrified. But the angel said to them, "Do not be afraid; for see—I am bringing you good news of great joy for all the people: to you is born this day in the city of David a Savior, who is the Messiah, the Lord. This will be a sign for you: you will find a child wrapped in bands of cloth and lying in a manger." And suddenly there was with the angel a multitude of the heavenly host, praising God and saying, "Glory to God in the highest heaven, and on earth peace among those whom he favors!"*

—Luke 2:8–14

# Messenger

*Y*ou stand there agape, wondering at me, half asleep among your sheep. You think you dream. I have spoken to many in their dreams, but not tonight. Tonight I am before you. Shall I sing to you with light and color? Shall I thunder, breaking the very rocks you stand on? You grovel. My message to you is lost. You see me with terror and awe. The glory that surrounds me blinds you to what I bring to you.

It is the glory of the One that shines so. The glory from which sprang all that is. The glory from which you came. That is the glory I reflect. For I stand in the presence of the One. The Holy One is my focus and my identity.

Yet tonight, tonight all of the glory and song, all of the light and power is nothing, nothing compared to the trembling, frail gift that comes to your world.

I shall tell you a story with my song. You love beginnings and endings. So . . .

In the beginning, there was the One.

And in that there is no need or imperfection. (Or should I say was? Tense is such a strange thing . . .) Yet

1

in all that completeness, something moved, and creation sprang from the hand of the One. It grew and became space and time and matter, suns and planets and pulsars.

And life—ah, life, there is a glory. Consider the sheep you nurture and the lice on your heads, the wolves you fear and the offspring you treasure. Life! So much more than stuff and space. Life!

But I am not done, for there is more. Listen . . .

In that beginning, there in the One. . . . Was . . . yes, was. . . . In that beginning, there in the One was . . . this. This night and all its tender paradox, this night that gives all and offers more, this night of light that shines in darkness. This night of silence that sings, this night that rejoices in tears. In this night it all comes clear.

Listen!

There is no other song or truth. You, you who gape and grovel, you will find a child, frail, born of a girl, frightened, to a husband, worried, in your world, confused.

And as you look upon that child, know this: As his mother holds him close, and comforts him with hand and breast, all of heaven holds its breath and weeps in wonder and in love.


So it is I sing to you, born in pain, alive in fear, doomed to die. Go and see!

So it is the song I sing is one of wonder and of joy, for heaven and earth are joined this night. The Creator, glory upon glory, bends down to be among you, like you, of you. Go and see!

And so it is that I, messenger of the One, sing to you.

For unto us a child is born.

*In that region there were shepherds living in the fields, keeping watch over their flock by night. Then an angel of the Lord stood before them, and the glory of the Lord shone around them, and they were terrified. But the angel said to them, "Do not be afraid; for see—I am bringing you good news of great joy for all the people: to you is born this day in the city of David a Savior, who is the Messiah, the Lord. This will be a sign for you: you will find a child wrapped in bands of cloth and lying in a manger." And suddenly there was with the angel a multitude of the heavenly host, praising God and saying, "Glory to God in the highest heaven, and on earth peace among those whom he favors!" When the angels had left them and gone to heaven, the shepherds said to one another, "Let us go now to Bethlehem and see this thing that has taken place, which the Lord has made known to us." So they went with haste and found Mary and Joseph, and the child lying in the manger.*

—Luke 2:8–20

# Common Man

*I* work for a living. The events of the world, who's running things, whether or not we've got our own king, what's right, what's wrong, none of that really matters, at least to me. Whoever's in charge, they'll expect me to do the work that keeps them in fine wool garments and mutton. Right and wrong have nothing to do with it. I am expected to do my work, and they sit in luxury and tell me that it's for my own good. I work for their living. No matter what my belief about God or demons, the sheep need water and food and protection. Sheep aren't the smartest animals. They need a lot of attention. That's my life, most of it anyway. People who live in the city, people like you, don't understand what I do. It's not like I can finish for the day and go home. In some ways this is my home, with the woolly idiots. They know me. They trust me. They

5

can pick my voice out of a marketplace of voices. I've seen a flock stampeded by lightning come to the call of a shepherd. They come to him because he was there every day, leading them, caring for them, healing them, protecting them, sharing what they live with. So I work for their living, too. That's funny. Kings and sheep have something in common. Me? Kings don't think I'm important. Sheep do. But then, what do sheep know?

I never felt that what I did mattered much. People who matter, important people, don't have to get their hands dirty. They pay for the privilege of letting others work for their living. They stay above it all. But one advantage we have, we who don't matter much—we don't have much to worry about. Just the basics. So I work. I do my job. And my life goes on. I do what needs doing for the sheep. I watch the stars at night. I drink some wine when I can come up with the money and put up with the headache. That December was cold. It had rained less than usual and some of us were worried about over-grazing the fields close to our hometown. That's Bethlehem. So we'd combined our flocks and led them up in the hills to the west of the town, to give the nearer pastures a rest.

We had a little more food and wine than usual to keep warm. We'd gathered wood and built a fire. For midwinter we were having a fine time. As usual, we talked in the night—almost as if the darkness released us, let us be something more than dust blown around by the things important people worry about. The taxation was on everyone's mind. Partly because we were worried about how much it would cost us, but more because of all the people on the move. Strange people from all sorts of places were wandering through and to Bethlehem. They might be distant relatives, but we laughed at how lost and upset some of them were. Pathetic. They seemed dazed, uprooted, dumb like the woolly idiots. You have to understand this was not a compliment from us. We laughed and then laughed louder when Ruben said sheep smelled better. There were a few more comments I won't repeat, but we began to wind down. It had been a long day. Getting such a large flock, unused to being together, to go into strange territory was no picnic. We were all tired and hoarse from yelling to each other and at them.

We had decided to set a watch. There were too many things we were unsure of to be very trusting. Strange country, strange flocks, strangers on the road. So we took turns watching. I never have trouble sleeping. And sleep I did. I woke and saw Isaac's foot near me. He hadn't said anything, just came and stood next to me. It was enough to wake me. I stood and settled my cloak about my shoulders, picked up my staff and set off a distance, away from the banked fire as Isaac took my place next to it. He never has trouble sleeping, either.

The stars are different in the hills. They're alive. There are so many more of them. It was the stars that showed me something was different. I realized I couldn't see them as well toward the west. It was as if dawn was coming. In the west?

Such light is not natural. And that can only mean trouble. I waited to make sure I wasn't seeing things, or dreaming, but it brightened, it grew. I walked back to the fire and my approach added to the change in the sound of the flock and roused the rest. We moved toward the light, gripping our staves. But each in his own way knew that that much light meant something we could do little about. It must have been an army to light the sky like that. What could shepherds do against an army? But worse, why an army, here in the hills, away from any road? And how could they be silent? There was no noise, only the wind and the sound of our breathing and the bleating of the sheep that woke, as confused as we were.

The light grew. I know no other way to describe it than a small dawn. It remained night around us but the brightness increased constantly, becoming focused in one spot that drew our eyes and our fears. Whatever was coming would come into view there at the crest of that hill. It was a hundred yards from us.

When he came into view—I think it was a he—it made less sense than before we could see him. The light came from him. At first it was hard to look straight at him, it was so bright, as if he'd swallowed a chunk of the sun. He kept coming; I'm not sure if he walked or floated. But he came toward us. He carried no weapons. He wore no armor. He was no warrior. But there was power there. The sheep froze as if they had no throats or legs. We were much the same. We had no choice but to watch and wait. I heard Ruben whimper like a child.

Time became very strange as he approached. He stopped and looked at us. I have no idea for how long. He just looked. His first words were foolish, appropriate perhaps, but foolish:

"Fear not!"

What were we supposed to do? Fear not! Here we stood looking at . . . looking at something that was so far beyond anything that we could understand or accept and he tells us to fear not. Foolishness. What did he expect us to do? It was not as if he did anything to make us afraid. It was just that what he was didn't fit into anything of our world. It makes me shiver to remember it. I felt smaller and more . . . I don't know, more human, more mortal than at any time in my life. This person, this being, was different than us. He looked like us. He had a face and hair, hands and legs. He was bigger, taller, and broader to match, but that wasn't the difference. It was as if he was made of different stuff. I can't imagine touching him.

He seemed to speak in words, but I could almost see

what he said. I cannot tell you everything I saw. He spoke of creation and our journey with God. I could see God's pain and sorrow. Imagine that. I never knew God was affected by anything. I thought that's what it meant to be God. But the messenger—that's what he was—an angel, told us of much I never knew or imagined. And beneath it all was joy. As if all the other, the making and promising and hoping and waiting and sorrowing, as if all of that, everything up till now was an introduction. And now was the joy. "Good news of great joy, which shall come to all people." I remember those words.

He painted his pictures, he spoke and we saw the news, the family in the stable, the child born to us, just as the prophet had said. And the joy flowed around us. Ahhh . . . It is something I will never forget. We hung there swimming in the moment as he spoke. But I think there was too much joy for him to contain. The sky exploded. Suddenly he was not alone. There was too much light to see. There was too much song to hear. There was too much of everything for anything except . . . I guess they call it awe.

"Glory to God!" they sang. They flew. They breathed. They danced. Glory.

And then Peace. Peace on earth for anyone willing to have it. Glory and Peace.

So we went. We left the flocks. We ran. It didn't feel as if we were leaving them. There was no tug. There was only one thing we could do. We went to the source of the joy.

At the stable there was no blazing light. There was no terror of something from somewhere else. There was a father, protective and concerned about us. Who were we? When we managed to tell him of the angels, instead of looking at us like crazy people, he grew quiet and stood aside. Then there was the mother. She was just a girl. Away from home, without family around her, she received us with a grace beyond her years. She was no stranger to angels either. She told us. Yes, we were in the right place. An angel had spoken to her.

Then there was the baby. Now, I'm not one to spend much time or attention on babies. This child was a baby boy. He didn't glow. I touched him. He was made of stuff like us. I mean he wasn't like the angel. But somehow I felt that being near him was what I was born for. I know that sounds crazy. But I wanted to sit there and look forever.

Peace and goodwill, the angel said. And here it was. But we couldn't stay. They had to rest. So, we left and returned to the woolly idiots.

They were all there. They'd been so frightened they stayed together. Or maybe, maybe, maybe somebody or something took care of them. Watched over them. Convinced them to stay together and wait for their shepherds. I don't know if an angel did that. They seem . . . beyond that or something. But now I know God can do all kinds of things.

That baby was like us. He wasn't beyond or above us. That's more of a wonder to me than if he'd been . . . different. But he was just like us. A common man. I wonder if he'll work for a living.

*Now the birth of Jesus the Messiah took place in this way.*
*When his mother Mary had been engaged to Joseph, but before*
*they lived together, she was found to be with child from the*
*Holy Spirit. Her husband Joseph, being a righteous man and*
*unwilling to expose her to public disgrace, planned to dismiss*
*her quietly. But just when he had resolved to do this, an angel*
*of the Lord appeared to him in a dream and said, "Joseph, son*
*of David, do not be afraid to take Mary as your wife, for the*
*child conceived in her is from the Holy Spirit. She will bear a*
*son, and you are to name him Jesus, for he will save his people*
*from their sins." . . . When Joseph awoke from sleep, he did as*
*the angel of the Lord commanded him; he took her as his wife,*
*but had no marital relations with her until she had borne a son;*
*and he named him Jesus.*

—Matthew 1:18–25

# Father

*H*ow can they do it? We're supposed to be the stronger
ones. Yet I know no man who could stand the pain and the
pressure. And they consider these children blessings.
They oooh and aaah over them like treasures of gold and
jewels, these burdens that they carry and then bear in discomfort and pain.

There comes another contraction. It pushes to be born.

It eases. At least it did not come on the road. That would
have been disaster. And this is not a bad place, warm from
the animals and plenty of clean straw. She accepts it as a
blessing, all of it. Where did she get this strength? She is
young, far from home and family. This is her first, and only
me to be a midwife. I know how to shape wood and make
furniture. I can put together pieces to create something
new. But I am beyond my depth here. She has told me
we are partners in all of this. She has told me that I am a

13

blessing that God has given to her. I think this God takes grand risks with young girls and carpenters. I think . . .

What does it matter what I think? All my plans and dreams were torn down months ago. Everything I planned—a safe home, a secure wife, strong children—all of it is changed. We are left with a stable in a strange town, a girl who bears a child sired by an angel, who is destined to be . . . something different than a carpenter.

It was all so clear, and good, and I had such hopes. They may not have been the hopes of kings or prophets, but they were mine. And she fit them well. It was a good match. She was pleased, as far as I could tell. But then . . . How am I to speak or even think of it? She told me, and all the hopes and plans shattered like some fragile cup on the hard rock of this child.

I was not reasonable at first. At least not what I consider reasonable. I have been called patient. It is no virtue I can claim. It is part of my grain, the way I am put together. But when she told me of the child I left her and walked into the hills, speaking to the wind like some madman. It took a while for me to calm down. And then I confess, I sat and cried for a time. It was hard to lose so much in one moment. Like a storm it broke out and through me. First the wind and then the rain.

But like any storm it blew itself out. And finally I sat and considered something other than myself She would bear the worst burden. I made up my mind to help her as best I could, not to make more trouble for her and the child she would bear. I resolved not to seek punishment for the breaking of the covenant of betrothal and to help her quietly. Once I decided that, I went home.

I slept, and I dreamed. And everything changed again.

Another contraction. She is sweating. Here, I can dry her forehead. She squeezes my hand. You wouldn't think such a small girl could grip that hard.

It is exhausting, not knowing what is dependable and what is going to be changed. I cannot say clearly how I knew the truth of the dream. It was as if the angel was there speaking to me. Not that I should trust angels after what had happened. But I woke knowing this was more than any of us understood.

Except perhaps her. She knew and understood with her heart more than all of us. Perhaps that's why she was chosen to bear the child. I told her that on the road on a day when the traveling was hard. I knew she suffered. And then she pointed out some wildflowers by the road. I gathered them and gave them to her. I told her she was a wonder and full of strength and faith that put me to shame.

She smiled, put her hand on my shoulder and told me not to forget that I'd been chosen too. That the child would need a father to show him how to be a man. She may as well have hit me with one of my hammers. It had never occurred to me. I would be raising this . . . child.

How do you raise the child of God? How do you teach him, when he is connected to the one who created everything? How do you show him what's right and wrong? How do you . . . Do you see my problem?

I considered this for days. Walking on the dusty road, in front of that donkey carrying her, as she carried the child.

It pushes again. It is stronger now. The time is near. She cannot bear much more of this. Or maybe it is I that cannot. She has born all of this mess with more balance and peace than I was able to command. There . . . it eases again.

This evening, just outside Bethlehem, she finally asked me what it was I mulled and muttered about. And I told her. I do not believe in hiding behind silence. She smiled again. And she told me that was something I would have to work out. She could be his mother, but I would have to be his father. She could teach him many things, but she could not teach him how to be a man. I knew, with her, that it would be a boy. I had seen it in the dreams. But we were beyond dreams now.

As we approached the town, I knew that whether God had chosen well or not, it was up to me to help this child, this boy child, to grow up to be a man. God can do anything God wishes. That's what makes God who God is. But perhaps there is something to being a man that God needs help with. Perhaps this boy will need a trade to support himself and teach him the discipline of work. Wood can teach humility. You must respect it for what it is. You are its partner in creating. Yes . . . perhaps there is something I can teach this child.

She bears down. It is coming now. He is coming now. He is here. He cries. May it be his worst grief. And it is a boy.

I shall name him Jesus. This child of Mary's, this child of God's, this child of mine.

*In those days a decree went out from Emperor Augustus that all
the world should be registered. . . . All went to their own towns
to be registered. Joseph also went from the town of Nazareth in
Galilee to Judea, to the city of David called Bethlehem,
because he was descended from the house and family of David.
He went to be registered with Mary, to whom he was engaged
and who was expecting a child. While they were there, the time
came for her to deliver her child. And she gave birth to her
firstborn son, and wrapped him in bands of cloth, and laid him
in a manger, because there was no place for them in the inn.*
—Luke 2:1–7

# Host

*I*'ve always considered myself a responsible citizen. I
believe that good neighbors are the key to a strong community. Running an inn is a tough business, and keeping
the people that live nearby from hating the sight of the
innkeeper is even harder. The clientele are not always
well behaved, especially after a little too much wine. You
can't blame most of them. They're away from home,
lonely. They want to have something other than loneliness. They come to the inn because they have no family
in town, or their family won't have them. And there's got
to be some good reason for that. So some of them drink
wine to soften their lot. I escort them away or bed them
down. Not only for their own good, but for the good of
the neighborhood. I try to be fair. It's good business.
Good business makes a strong community.

This whole census thing was crazy. Don't get me wrong,
it was good for business. The peace that the Romans
brought has been a good thing—more travel, more travelers, more business, good for the community. But the census ordered by Augustus . . . the whole world . . . I don't

mean to be critical of Caesar, but that was a little much. People had to come home to register, some who lived days and days away. Not all had relatives to stay with. And it took time to register. The lines of people . . . But added to that were those going to other places, passing through Bethlehem. It seemed the whole world was on the move. Everybody was hurrying to go somewhere, and it seemed they all wanted to stay at my inn. Excuse me.

Simeon! Did you clean out the stable? Well, get to it.

Sorry. If I don't follow them around, well, you know . . .

Let's see . . . Oh, the census. There were total strangers sleeping in the same beds, which happened anyway sometimes, but three in the same bed? There were fights and complaints, complaints, complaints. The neighbors went crazy. I guess they needed someone to yell at, all the strangers in town and the problems they brought with them. In my profession you have to learn how to take people's anger. Most of the time they don't mean anything by it anyway. So I keep an open door and a smile on my face. Or at least I try to. That's my job, no matter how crazy it gets.

It had been a brutal day. A knife fight at breakfast and three drunks for supper. I'd rented every bed to someone and had finally lain down on a table. I can sleep anywhere. I thought I was dreaming when I heard the knock on the door. More like having a nightmare. More trouble. Only trouble comes in the middle of the night. This was too much.

I threw back the bolt and pulled the door open with not a trace of my smile anywhere. Neighbor or traveler, there was a limit. Business and community were beside the point. I had had it. I had given, given, given, rushed and scrambled, tried to be nice in the face of it all, and look at all the wonderful thanks I received; someone pounding on my door in the middle of a night half gone. If God was in his heaven, where was his justice? What did I do to deserve this?

The man who received the brunt of my anger was in no shape to take it. He wasn't sick or injured or drunk, just tired from traveling. Who wasn't these days? But this poor soul had a problem. That was obvious. He looked at my face, saw my anger, and looked back out to the street. There stood a donkey with its head down. And on it a young woman. A very pregnant young woman. How do you stay angry at a lady who's going to have a baby? I turned back to the nervous father-to-be. I remember my first . . . Well, that's another story.

"Do you have any room? Her time is near."

My hand hid my face as I went through every possibility. There were no rooms. That was the long and the short of it. They couldn't stay in the public room. If she were to deliver . . . No, not there. My room was filled. Where was there space for them? Of course!

"There's no room in here." He looked like I'd hit him. "But follow me. Come on, I don't think there's much time to waste." My inn is built next to the hill. Behind the building is the cave we use for the animals. We've enlarged it, taken out the shaky parts, smoothed the rough corners. To tell you the truth, I go there sometimes on chilly days to nap in the straw. Anyway, he hesitated only a moment and then, like a thirsty horse smelling water, followed, pulling the donkey behind him.

As we got her off the animal, I saw so many thoughts and feelings go through him. But the one that settled was so rare that I was left without words. And let me tell you that is rare. He stood looking at me with sympathy and understanding. I got the feeling he actually knew and appreciated something more than what he was getting from me. I've thought about this since. At the time I stood there and didn't know what to say.

He looked around and said simply, "Yes, a stable. The Lord provides for His own."

I helped them get settled and went to get my wife. It was clear that the woman was in labor. But Joseph, that was his name, he helped her. It was done before my wife and I returned.

In the midst of that crazy, rushed, complicated world, without sleep and with little comfort, they all seemed at home, at peace. I stood there looking at them and didn't notice there were tears in my eyes until my wife reached out and touched my face. The Lord provided for His own and on that night it seemed He was providing for all of us. He was providing peace. He was providing a home, a family. It made all the hurry and hassle seem less crazy and more worthwhile. He was showing me what I was working so hard to offer to all the world—a safe place to rest along the way, a safe place with more rooms than I thought there were.

I was lucky . . . blessed, you could say. But all of us have corners where we can make room. We all have at least one place in our lives that could be such safe places. Our lives are filled with grumpy travelers and worried neighbors and we are all exhausted from trying to be nice, for whatever reason, nice to a world that is in too much of a hurry to care. But now and then we can be a blessing.

Listen to me. I sound like a rabbi.

They left the next morning. They found family in town—relatives, I mean. But I will never forget them. They filled up much more than my stable . . .

Speaking of which, Simeon! Simeon! Where did he get to now?

Oh, nice talking to you. Hope you come again. You'll always be welcome here.

*In the time of King Herod, after Jesus was born in Bethlehem of
Judea, wise men from the East came to Jerusalem, asking,
"Where is the child who has been born king of the Jews? For
we observed his star at its rising, and we have come to pay him
homage." When King Herod heard this, he was frightened, and
all Jerusalem with him; and calling together all the chief
priests and scribes of the people, he inquired of them where the
Messiah was to be born. They told him, "In Bethlehem of
Judea; for so it has been written by the prophet. . . . Then Herod
secretly called for the wise men and learned from them the
exact time when the star had appeared. Then he sent them to
Bethlehem, saying, "Go and search diligently for the child; and
when you have found him, bring me word so that I may also go
and pay him homage." When they had heard the king, they set
out; and there, ahead of them, went the star that they had seen
at its rising, until it stopped over the place where the child was.
When they saw that the star had stopped, they were over-
whelmed with joy. On entering the house, they saw the child
with Mary his mother; and they knelt down and paid him homage. Then, opening their treasure chests, they offered him gifts
of gold, frankincense, and myrrh. And having been warned in a
dream not to return to Herod, they left for their own country by
another road.*

—Matthew 2:1–12

# One of the Wise

*T*hey call me one of the wise. A title that is flattering
until one considers what wisdom implies. Many years
ago my teacher told me, "If one is to be truly wise, one
must seek humility." Flattery evaporates as the misty nonsense it is in the hard light of that truth. Rather than one
who is wise, I would prefer to be known as one who
seeks. And once, one who was found.

I read the heavens. It is a gift, a talent. Even as a child I
used to roam through the stars, like the celestial wanderers,

the bright lights that drift like errant sheep through the rest of the flock. My parents thought me strange in the head until an old man, dressed in fine robes, came one day to my father in the bazaar and asked to meet me. He was clearly a man of means and power, though humble of demeanor. He spoke to my parents with respect and asked if they would apprentice me to him to be a philosopher and reader of the heavens. When they hesitated he told them he had come because it had been written in those same heavens that my fate was to be great among those who read the hand of God. I would be remembered and called wise by humankind long after the towers of our world were dust. And then he told them to say nothing of this to me, knowing not that I listened to every word. After a time they called me from my perch in the loft and told me I would go with this man to be educated. My mother cried. My father gave me fatherly advice, turned, and left. My teacher brought me here where I write this these seventy years later. His home became my home and he, he remained my teacher until the day he told me my fate. He also spoke of my loneliness.

He said, almost in a whisper, "You know so much of the heavens. You see so much. Yet you miss so much. Do not forget the stars were made for warmth. Do not fear being touched, my boy." And with such cryptic words he died as he had lived—quietly and with great respect for the Giver of the gift of life. My master left me on that day to wander and seek alone. I thought of his words, but did not worry over them. I was occupied.

I became well known for the accuracy with which I read the heavens, but I was never what you might call popular. I read what I see. The truth is not always easy or simple or what people want to hear. So I gained a reputation but no great following.

What do I read? I read what is written for me to read.

I study the ascension and declination, the position of this against that, and in the studying I see through to what is to be. It is cold and hard and real. In many ways that truth out there is more real for me than the troublesome reality here below the stars. It has kept me alone much of my life, isolated from human warmth by the fire of the stars. They have always led me away from people. Except once.

When I was younger, I cursed my gift. Sometimes I yearned for the warmth of human touch. But I knew even in my anger and frustration that to turn away from this capability would be to deny truth, to turn from what really is. That would be a folly, spelling destruction to all I hold precious. When I gaze there at the black tablet of the heavens and see the fine fire of the night, glittering and shining across that page, I feel filled, filled with the very light of the stars. As if they shone in me. Oh bother. Words are useless. So, curse it I might, but deny it? Never.

Besides, I waited for my fate. It was a lure that kept me gazing. I was curious. What would I see? What great truth would be written there for me to read? I witnessed many celestial events, many movements of history, and still I waited.

In my forty-seventh year, on an early spring night, I had the first inkling of what was to be. It seemed all the heavens held still in expectation and awe. You smile. Well, you have not the stars for companions. And how it shone, not a blazing brightness, but new, a new star conceived in heaven's womb. A bit to the south and west of the zenith. I felt it draw me, as iron filings are drawn to a lodestone. I knew it was my fate glimmering there. I weighed it in my mind and heart and felt no dread, no fear, no earth-rattling shift in the balances. But undeniably the message was written and it was mine to read.

As I read, I gathered maps of the west and writings of their humble seekers. In my wanderings I had learned there is wisdom in every land. But the scrolls could not hold me. The new star's growing brilliance spoke more clearly. It was more articulate than the writings. And the dreams. Oh, the brightness of the dreams. They cascaded into my small mind as a flood runs into a narrow ravine. A flood of the light and the music of the stars. . . . I saw them then as troublesome and distracting. I know now they were part of something so grand it could not be contained in what was to be seen with the eyes and heard with the ears.

I am an old fool.

It was late summer when Caspar and Melchior came. Each to ask about the star and what they read written there. They came to me, Belshazar the truth teller. They came because they, too, were drawn by their fate.

Caspar financed the expedition that each of us knew must be made. We did not argue over that. He had the money, and to spare. What we most worried over was the matter of gifts. We knew it was a king—a great ruler of such stature that the wealth and power of all the emperors of the earth would be dust while this one still reigned. The problem being: what does one bring as a gift to such power and glory? We studied and meditated and discussed and, I must admit, argued over it. Three such private people having to make a joint venture was not an easy thing, and I suppose the arguing was how we took out the tension.

Caspar held out for good old gold. But truly it is the gift of kings. Its very color symbolizes power and influence and value. So we left that to him. Melchior was the artist. We wanted to express what seemed to be a thread of grace and loveliness that shone through the star. He came back to my house one day in early September fairly dancing. "It will be incense, sweet smelling, carrying mood and meditation up to the gods." So frankincense was his. They were both appalled by my choice of myrrh. "The king is just born. He will reign forever. You can read it better than we. Why do you bring a gift of funeral spice?" But as we prepared to leave I was silent. And finally they shook their heads and went on packing.

The trip was uneventful. Interesting, but uneventful. We followed what we saw written. We were unanimous in our direction, and as we traveled, we eliminated options until it was clear that Rome's province of Judea was our destination. We were a bit uneasy at that. The people of that land have a reputation for scorning ones of our calling. It seems their God is a jealous god and will not abide the divination we practice. They see us as charlatans, confidence men with nothing in mind but cheating people of their money.

On the other hand, I had perused some of their prophets, and had found there some who spoke of a relationship with their god that made sense to me. I had never much paid attention to the gods. But these holy men made sense. I respected their judgments. I also had felt in some of these writings a resonance with what I read in the heavens. I felt a sense of intimacy and closeness unknown in any of the gods of whom I had heard, a sense of freedom and a terrible, wonderful purpose being worked out in the birth of the king whose star directed us. But I dismissed that as an emotional reaction. I had much to learn.

Another reason we dreaded Judea was Herod, its king. Our conference with him was unsettling at best. But his readers of wisdom gave us further direction. When he told us to return to him that he might worship the king, my skin crawled. He resembled a spider too much for my liking. Spiders worship nothing except their own appetites. And his was voracious.

So, finally, we came to Bethlehem. The birth had occurred some time before, but the star—my fate—still shone brightly. And it gave us what direction we needed, for by this time each of us walked as in a dream. It was as if there was something more than the position and relation of the stars that guided us. No matter how I tried to deny it and put it aside, this sense of being guided was overwhelming.

When we found the lodging of the family, and brought the gifts to them, all groveled before us and seemed unreal in their mistake. They attended *us* when in their midst was the one of which the very heavens sang. We came in silence, unannounced. Yet the family—mother, father and child—seemed to expect us, or at least were not surprised when three weary, bearded travelers came parading into their dwelling carrying extravagant gifts for a carpenter's baby boy. We were wildly inappropriate in our presence by any standard of behavior imaginable. Yet we all knew, we magi and that family, that there was something else afoot here. Something that made our kneeling before the infant the only possible behavior.

When it was my turn to present my gift to the child, I came with the myrrh, placing the flask at the feet of his mother, my forehead on the dirt floor. I named my gift and started to explain it, but choked on the tears that stopped my words and blinded me. I rose and looked into the mother's eyes and, through my tears, saw hers. Then I knew that she knew his fate just as I did. I had read it in the stars. She had felt it with the intuition of a mother's heart. I gave the gift of funeral spice because I had seen that this child, now held close and secure at his mother's breast, would one day be both loved and despised. He would speak and act in ways that would shake the world. And he would be betrayed and tortured and killed because of the truth he bore.

I could not face her after that, after she had seen into my heart, and known my sadness and weariness with a world that destroys its best. I wished to return to the cold fire of the distant stars and their unfailing clarity. But she lifted the child to me. And that sight has haunted me until this day. For I saw in that child my own humanity. I saw my own loneliness. And I saw my own hope. You see, the best beloved of all creation found me out. My gift to him, my giving of his fate to him, has tied me to him and his all-too-human life . . . and will not let me escape, no matter where I journey.

I still read the stars and the truth they tell, but because of what I received I see no uncaring random hand that writes, but one of mercy. Perhaps it always was so, and I, in my arrogance, in fear of my own need, refused to see the hand of God writing there.

I sit here now, an old man. I know the child's fate is completed this day. I read it in the stars. I know he finished what the Creator gave him to do. He has become a star: God's message, written in his cradle and on his cross, to guide us through the cold distances of loneliness to our own human need. To guide us home to the light of the one Creator's love.

So, am I wise? Perhaps. I do not seek humility any more. It finds me each time I remember and recognize the gift. For the King is born.

It is written in the stars.

*When Herod saw that he had been tricked by the wise men, he was infuriated, and he sent and killed all the children in and around Bethlehem who were two years old or under, according to the time that he had learned from the wise men. Then was fulfilled what had been spoken through the prophet Jeremiah: "A voice was heard in Ramah, wailing and loud lamentation, Rachel weeping for her children, because they are no more."*

—Matthew 2:16–18

# Arranger

*H*ow can you live when your heart has been murdered? How can you begin to trust again in life? How can anything hold beauty or joy when every day is filled with memories too painful to embrace? How can you love again when your love has been spilled onto the ground, like milk from a broken jug?

These are my litanies of grief. I recite them with my heart. There is never a response.

There is no sense of time spent or wasted. Time is tangled in a knot drawn so tight it squeezes all the sense out of my spirit. Hope only lives when we are able to allow this moment to live and breathe. I have no strength to allow me now to live. That soldier's sword cut away my strength and my hope. I am left, alone.

I could hate her. It is because of her child that the sword took my life. I have tried to hate her. But even that is too close to the center of my pain. She was fleeing when I last saw her. So I let her go, with her child.

But I remember. At least I can remember.

She and her husband came to Bethlehem in the dimness of a dying evening. They were pushed and shoved here because of Rome's desire to know how many it ruled. It is a beast and taxes are its fodder. Taxes and children. Those two came because of his family roots. We are distantly related.

But in that darkness they had no time to find their relatives. They needed shelter. She was in labor. I heard this later when I spoke with them, after my husband, Isaac, came to tell me of angels' light and song and to drag me to the stable behind the inn.

I took charge of them. Isaac knew I would, I was the one who always took charge, the arranger. I tried to bring some comfort to her, young and in a strange town as she was. Comfort. . . . My boy's name was Nahum. It means comforter . . ."

You see? I can remember. But all my memories come there, like paths that wind around a hill. No matter where I wander I come back to the pain. . . .

I arranged for them to move to Aunt Miriam's. She always knew how to make me feel safe and cared for. She held me in my darkness. It is one of the bits I remember from that day. She held me.

It was a good match, a widow and the new family. But that girl was unusual. I could tell. There was about her a sense of purpose and value. It was as if she knew she was valuable, as if she had a purpose that ran deeper than any plans or arrangements. She faced her situation with wide eyes, as if each moment was too important to let slide by without noticing.

I loved to talk with her. She would listen. I would find myself telling her things. . . . I wish she was here. Mary. That was her name. I told her . . . so much. She talked too. But it always felt as if what she told me did not take anything away from what I said or thought. As if her simple conversation in its cadence and rhythms, as she spoke and listened, was a dance to some music that was clean and good. And it left any who shared the dance with her refreshed.

She told me of the angel.

My life is populated with angels . . . Isaac, Mary, Death . . .

She told me of Joseph's dream.

One day I came carrying my common gifts of milk and cheese and bread. And there the camels stood, dressed like nobility. Servants stood in the street, dressed better than the camels but just as tired. They had swords . . .

I pushed into Aunt Miriam's house, afraid. I ran into another of the servants inside the door. The milk went all over him. I yelled and hit him. I remember how hard he was. But he was polite to a crazy madwoman. They all were. They all were quiet. As if their words would disturb much more than a child's sleep. Their wealth lay at Mary's feet.

It was the stars had brought them. Angels, dreams and stars . . .

They were gone the next morning. And Mary spoke to me in whispers of another dream.

"We have to go, Leah. Joseph had another dream. My boy is in danger."

I pitied her, driven by dreams. And I confess I envied her. What she had of angels' touch and stars' omens. All I had were children to chase and food to cook and rooms to clean and water to carry. She was part of a grand story and I, I stood in the roadway and watched them leave. She had gifts. All I had was . . .

I was a fool.

They came quickly. Isaac was with the sheep or I'm sure, . . . he would be with Nahum.

They came with drawn swords, two huge men that filled up my room before I knew they were at the door. It is as if I can see them before me. They had no shields. They didn't need them for this battle. Their eyes were dark with purpose but there was no passion there. They were killers. They were efficient.

I swung a pot. . . . I didn't think. It was at hand. As I

lifted it, one of them grasped my wrist. The pot fell and broke. And the other swung his sword.

Nahum never cried out. He was a good boy.

The silence of death is not frightening. It is a life of silence, weighed down by dark isolation. That is a horror. He was still, so still. He was broken. And I could not . . .

What is left? What is there to say?

How long has it been?

I remember Miriam holding me and weeping. I remember the pieces of the pot. I saved them to put them back together. They would not fit no matter how I tried. I remember strange details, bits and pieces of days and nights that rose to the surface of the dark broth of emptiness. And slipped away again, leaving me, alone.

The light is in my eyes. But I can see Isaac. He is standing in the setting sun against the door of our house. I remember him . . . He did . . . everything, when I could do nothing. He is so gentle. He has lost so much. And he is smiling, with shining eyes. They are listening. The children, golden in the twilight. They are . . . gifts. Precious. And they are listening to him.

It is the angel story. That is why he shines so.

There is so much to remember. There is so much pain. But there is so much . . . else. There is the horror, but there is the gift. And all the darkness cannot deny its light. I remember, as in a dream.

But perhaps it is time to wake. Perhaps it is time to let the angels and the stars and the dreams speak of the power of the gift. The gift that shines in the darkness and the darkness cannot overcome it. Nahum is part of that story. I am part of that story. "Isaac, I remember . . ."

*In the sixth month the angel Gabriel was sent by God to a town
in Galilee called Nazareth, to a virgin engaged to a man whose
name was Joseph, of the house of David. The virgin's name was
Mary. And he came to her and said, "Greetings, favored one!
The Lord is with you." But she was much perplexed by his
words and pondered what sort of greeting this might be. The
angel said to her, "Do not be afraid, Mary, for you have found
favor with God. And now, you will conceive in your womb and
bear a son, and you will name him Jesus. He will be great, and
will be called the Son of the Most High, and the Lord God will
give to him the throne of his ancestor David. He will reign over
the house of Jacob forever, and of his kingdom there will be no
end." Mary said to the angel, "How can this be, since I am a
virgin?" The angel said to her, "The Holy Spirit will come upon
you, and the power of the Most High will overshadow you;
therefore the child to be born will be holy; he will be called Son
of God. . . . For nothing will be impossible with God." Then
Mary said, "Here am I, the servant of the Lord; let it be with me
according to your word." Then the angel departed from her.*
—Luke 1:26–38

# Mother

*N*ow, I know you want to know what it was like to
receive this wonderful gift. But I'll warn you right from
the start, it may not be the story you expect. So many people ask me questions, but I get the feeling they want to
hear what they already have in their heads. I wonder if
they listen to me at all.

That nice young man Luke, so serious he is. The last
time he was here I told him to relax a little bit and enjoy
himself. After all, every day is a wonder. What good is the
gift if we never notice it? Anyway, he, I mean Luke, sat
here and wrote things down while I talked. Can you imagine that? He told me that people needed to know how it

all happened, that it would mean a lot to them and help them understand how important my boy was. I don't know. It's hard for me, even now, after all that's happened, to think of him as anything other than my boy, my baby boy. So you can see, you may not hear everything you want to. And you may hear things you didn't expect.

Luke, the young man who wrote things down, I don't think he was very pleased when I laughed about some of my memories. Just between you and me, I think he's going to leave some parts out. He got quite red in the face when I spoke about Joseph and how much we loved each other. I'm afraid I laughed when I saw his expression. What did he expect to hear me say? Joseph was such a good man, gentle and willing to listen. Even when what he heard was beyond belief Joseph appreciated the gift. He used to bring me wildflowers after the rains. I remember one day he came home with arms full of flowers. He . . . Well, now *I'm* blushing. But as I was saying, I don't think Luke will include any of that.

I'm sorry, what were we talking about? That's what you get when you talk to an old woman. I wander around like a sheep. But I can remember *then* so clearly. Now seems less clear than then. So what was I . . . oh yes, Joseph. We were betrothed to each other. I had no voice in the matter, but if the truth is told, I was very pleased with our match. He wasn't too old and he was strong. I'd seen him carrying timbers. He was a carpenter, you know. So as things went along I thought life was wonderful. Then the angel came.

Now don't you write anything down. Just listen. And stop looking at me as if I belonged in the Temple. It wasn't like that. Life is full of wonders. The dawn is so much of a wonder, it is hard for me to believe that people see it and still don't believe in God. It was strange, though. The angel, I mean. Angels are different. They're not like us.

It was winter, late winter, and he came in the darkness just before dawn. I felt him first. I didn't know it was the angel. It felt like a storm was coming. Quiet. The noises of the night stopped. I knew that I should go outside. I can't really tell you how or why. I just knew. I went out and there he was, Gabriel. I didn't know that then, but that's who it was. He bowed to me. He spoke to me with great respect. This I was not used to. Now it's not as if people kicked me around. My family was good to me. But he treated me as if I was more than one of the family or someone from the village. He *bowed!* I didn't think he was wrong. There was a rightness about him that put that thought right out of my head. But I got the feeling he knew something I didn't know. Why was I favored? That's what he called me, "Favored one."

That young man Luke shook his head when I told him about my trouble with the angel and what he told me. Why, anyone with half a mind would have wondered what was going on! Just because it's an angel doing the talking doesn't mean you stop using your sense. I told Luke that and he nodded. So I said "What? Why are you nodding?" He said, "The mother of our Lord was comfortable speaking with angels." I told him he had no more sense than the table he was writing on. That angel turned my life upside down. That angel changed every dream I ever had. Next time an angel tells you you're pregnant you just sit there and pray! Comfortable speaking with angels . . .

Gabriel was so different I don't know if anyone could be really comfortable with him. But I felt . . . good. I felt as if whatever God was asking of me was beautiful. I remembered all the stories from the Bible of the high and mighty being overturned by the small and insignificant. I remembered the power and the goodness of God, and I realized perhaps God's hopes and dreams for us were different than ours. Maybe I could have something to do with that.

Oh, I was so young. It was beautiful, but it was lonely and scary. I thought for sure I'd have to give up Joseph. But he told me he had a dream. And when my family sent me away to visit Cousin Elizabeth, she told me I was blessed. She knew. Somehow she knew about the gift. They all helped so much. But when it comes down to it there is little anyone can do for mothers. They have to do it themselves.

The trip to Bethlehem was awful. I was so pregnant I thought I'd die. Now you look like Luke. You think I should have floated down the road from Nazareth? I don't care how reasonable taxation is, or what prophesies there are in the Bible, that trip was awful. Poor Joseph had to worry about me and put up with me. At that point I wasn't very happy. I'm sure God forgives me, and us all in our weakness. That was the worst part. Every mile seemed another reason to suffer.

By the time we got there I *was* floating, in a haze of pain. There was no time to look for relatives. I was in labor. Joseph found us a place to bed down with the animals. I remember people helping me off the donkey and onto a bed of straw. The birth was hard work. It was my first. I didn't really know what to do. But I remembered that God was doing something, even with all of this strange discomfort and pain. And then he was there, crying, My boy.

Look at me, it still fills me up till I overflow. I leak like an old bucket. He was beautiful. Every baby is. But I saw in him a promise and a gift. So many had believed and sacrificed and worked to bring us along to here. My parents and Joseph and Elizabeth and the innkeeper and . . . God. And this baby was a result of all that promise and belief and sacrifice. He opened his little hands and made it worth it all. Not by doing anything, just by being. He was the perfect way of making it clear. I wish you could have seen him. You would have known what I meant.

The shepherds came. They were terrified and excited and like children, wanting to see and touch. They bowed to me, as Gabriel had. Silly men. Here lay the promise and the gift and they bowed to me. But somehow I knew that to turn down their worship would cheapen what they'd seen and heard. They went away reluctantly.

The Magi came later. They came on the star's schedule. And when they got there they hardly saw me. They knew something. They knew of his power and his glory, yes. But they knew of the price he would pay. Myrrh. A spice for embalming. They knew.

There was so much. There are so many memories. They crowd around me like angels calling me to come out and listen. Some of them are sweet like a dawn after rain. Some of them cut like a bolt of lightening in a dark night. It's sad. When I think of his hands I see both. I see his fat little baby hands reaching and grasping at new life. I see his callused hands, hurt and wounded, not reaching or grasping at all. I can't make one go away if I remember the other. They are both part of him and who he was. They are both part of how I knew him as his mother.

But I will tell you this. It is all part of the gift. Even the pain . . . even the pain. If he had lived above or beyond it, would he have meant so much to so many? That was the gift of him. My baby boy. The man on the cross. There I go, leaking again.

Did you ever wonder why God made butterflies? I never understood until I realized how much there was to life. It just goes on and on. Did you know they come from worms? Butterflies I mean. Maybe we'll do that. He did, you know. My boy. My baby boy.

Well, that's enough of my rambling. You listen to an old woman very well. It is a gift you know, to be a good listener. Thank you. Would you like some soup?

*On the third day there was a wedding in Cana of Galilee, and the mother of Jesus was there. Jesus and his disciples had also been invited to the wedding. When the wine gave out, the mother of Jesus said to him, "They have no wine." And Jesus said to her, "Woman, what concern is that to you and to me? My hour has not yet come." His mother said to the servants, "Do whatever he tells you." . . . Jesus said to them, "Fill the jars with water." And they filled them up to the brim. He said to them, "Now draw some out, and take it to the chief steward." So they took it. When the steward tasted the water that had become wine, [he] . . . called the bridegroom and said to him, "Everyone serves the good wine first, and then the inferior wine after the guests have become drunk. But you have kept the good wine until now."*

—John 2:1–11

# Father of the Groom

*I*'ve always prided myself on my ability to make do. No matter the situation, you can depend on me. I find a way. You learn to depend on yourself, to plan ahead, to put things aside to use when needed. People who brag are stupid. They aren't sure enough of what they've done. They need someone else to widen their eyes and nod and round their mouths in approval. I just believe in doing the job and doing it right.

It's rare when you can find someone to trust. Most of the time you're doing someone a favor by including them in your plans. Then you have to check up on them to make sure they don't get tangled in their own desire to impress you. It's twice as much work to have a helper. But that's why people come to me when they want something done. I make sure it happens, rather than looking for an excuse about why it didn't happen. You don't make extravagant claims ahead of time or behind time. They have a bad habit of biting you when you least expect it. Don't say much and make sure it happens the way it's supposed to.

My father taught me this. He would give me a job and stand back and watch. If I succeeded, I got another job. If I failed, I paid. No excuses. He told me his rod was less painful than what I would face after I grew. I learned to keep my counsel and get things done right, the first time.

When I grew and got a family of my own, I handled my household the same way. Everyone knew what to expect. Keep things clear and there are no misunderstandings. Family means responsibilities. All the more important to keep things in order and working correctly. Wives and children and servants and . . . house and . . . The list is long. But if you keep at it every day, making sure everything is in its place, correcting anything that isn't, it works. My household was orderly. That which wasn't—well, it changed or it didn't have a place there. I say *was*. That was before the wedding.

It was my son's time for marriage. I had arranged a good match. Her family had a good dowry. She seemed healthy and a good worker. I checked her teeth. The ones with bad teeth don't build healthy children. So I was satisfied. We planned the wedding feast. It would be appropriate.

Such events are the high points of community life. They are the landmarks that people use to remember time. "You know around the time of Elias's son's wedding, the year before the storm that knocked down the synagogue." Weddings, funerals, disasters, wars—they define the time of a community's life, as birth and death define the life of a family. The memory of the town is long. It holds the details of a celebration as part of its history. Food, wine, dancing, each is talked about and compared and judged. Each is held up against the expectations the community has for that family.

So as I planned, I took all this into account. I would not go overboard. Extravagance is wasteful and stupid. But this was a job that needed to be done correctly. Everything in its place, the appropriate measure. Elias's first son's wedding would be remembered, well.

To accomplish this I knew I had to cover the details myself. There would be no excuses or shortfalls. There would be no last-minute hair pulling. I would provide the steward with a comfortable margin in every category, well thought out and planned. The whole affair would be an example of order.

I didn't count on a roof collapsing. It was the bugs. They ate away a rafter in the storeroom, and down came the roof on the amphora, the night before the wedding feast. I must confess I lost my temper. I kicked one servant right through the doorway. After I'd calmed down, I took note what had been broken. Two jars of wine that were for the wedding, and three of vinegar that I was selling next week. We would still have enough. I had planned with some margin.

The feast was in full swing when the steward came to me, red-faced. He mumbled and stumbled and finally blurted out that we were nearly out of wine. I called him a fool and went with him back into the storeroom. The large jars stood there, three more full. I told him he wasn't worth his keep if he couldn't use his eyes better. "But sir, these are vinegar." The roof had destroyed *five* jars of wine.

I had made a mistake.

In the shade and sour smell of that room I leaned back against the wall. My father's rod was nothing compared to the consequences of this. "Remember, that was the year Elias ran out of wine." "Before you do business with him you might want to know that he ran out of wine at his son's wedding feast. He couldn't tell the difference between wine and vinegar." "Poor Elias, he didn't count on all those ants coming to the feast. They drank all his wine." I could hear laughter.

The laughter in my imagination dissolved into the laughter of the party, still going on. The shortfall was unknown. For how long? The steward had left the room, probably in fear. I came out into the brightness, squinting in the light. I had no idea what to do. For all my planning, for all my ability to make things work, I had failed. Excuses don't count. I felt like a child, shamed and trapped by my own weakness.

As my eyes adjusted to the light, I saw the steward speaking with the carpenter's widow. Her son was with her. They seemed to be arguing. The steward looked at her as if she were mad. Her son shook his head and raised his eyes to the bright sky. He shrugged. She seemed in total control of the situation. I had always made it a policy to avoid such women. She had summoned servants and they brought empty wine jars. They brought my shame to the well. At her direction they filled them with water. The steward had given up and her son followed behind, resigned to her authority.

The sun seemed brighter suddenly. I bent my head and shaded my eyes. I felt a light breeze, full of fragrance. When I looked up, the steward was lifting a cup to his lips. The carpenter's widow peered up at him. His eyes grew wide. He stood there silent, shaking his head like someone trying to wake from a dream. One of the guests, John the tanner, came up behind and stuck out his cup. "Time to bring out the cheap stuff, eh?" He not only smelled bad, he was rude. The steward looked at the widow, she nodded, and he poured John's cup full.

The rest is town history. My shame became my praise. My mistake became a new benchmark in generosity and good planning. "Remember, it was the year of Elias's feast, the one with the wonderful wine. He saved the best for last. Knows how to throw a party, he does."

But I knew. It had nothing to do with my planning or my wisdom or my capability. I was blessed. There, by my well, in the midst of my shame and failure, the sun had shone, the breeze had blown, and Mary and her son had changed everything that I depended on. They brought something into my life that did not run out even after the wine was gone.

So things are different. I am different. Perhaps I am a bit less dependable, less sure of myself. But I have something I never knew. For the sun, for the breeze, for the water and the wine and for the widow and her son, for the miracle and the celebration of life, I am grateful. After all, the best is yet to come.

Would you like a cup of wine?

*He left . . . and entered their synagogue; a man was there with
a withered hand, and they asked him, "Is it lawful to cure on
the sabbath?" so that they might accuse him. He said to them,
"Suppose one of you has only one sheep and it falls into a pit
on the sabbath; will you not lay hold of it and lift it out? How
much more valuable is a human being than a sheep! So it is
lawful to do good on the sabbath." Then he said to the man,
"Stretch out your hand." He stretched it out, and it was
restored, as sound as the other. But the Pharisees went out and
conspired against him, how to destroy him. When Jesus became
aware of this, he departed. Many crowds followed him, and he
cured all of them. . . .*

—Matthew 12:9–15

# Beggar

*I* have a withered hand. It was crushed when I was a boy.
A simple moment of curiosity changed my life. Two
stones, a shiny something in the shadow between them. I
reached and they slipped, grinding the life out of my
small arm. I never did get to the shiny something.

Don't get me wrong. I'm not complaining. What good
would it do? I make a decent living as a beggar. Do not
look down your nose at me. I hurt no one. All these years
I have brought in enough money to buy food and clothes
and make do. It is a business. Others dig in the dirt; I help
people feel good about their own health. It is a skill.
There is an order to my world, rules and laws that make
things work. Always be pathetic enough to help them see
how much you need. Never be disgusting enough to make
them avoid you. Always put yourself in a place where
they have to pass you closely, so they can't avoid your
infirmity. Never block their passage or be so loud in your
pleading that they can condemn you. Always help them

feel guilt for your infirmity and their health. Never try to make them responsible for your well-being—they will avoid that at all costs. Always live humbly. If they see that you have anything nice they will think you don't deserve pity. Never trust them to give today if they gave before. People are not dependable.

You see? It is a business I learned as a child and I developed into a fairly good beggar as I grew. But one can never forget the rules. That is what makes life livable. That's how we defend ourselves from being crushed by all the horrors that make up nightmares.

That's partly why I tell this story. Because of the healer. There've been stories about him circulating for a while now. Who knows which ones are true? Some scoff at the idea of being able to heal the sick. A trick, they say. But I was there. I saw it happen. He broke the rules.

My best begging spot is near the synagogue. People like to give on the way to pray because they think God will listen better to their prayers. They are beggars in their own way and think if they follow the rules things will work better. Who knows? Or they give after their prayers because they feel guilty or grateful. I prefer the guilty because I can manipulate them better. But grateful people tend to give more. The trouble with gratitude is that it doesn't last. Remember the rule about not trusting them? Well, there you have it.

Anyway, everyone knows that's where I stay, near the synagogue. On the Sabbath I don't say much of anything. I want people to think I'm not working. Can't break the law. I merely show my arm, smashed and withered up as it is and it speaks for itself. Another of those rules.

He came with a crowd on that Sabbath. We'd heard about him. We'd heard he was saying all kinds of things, causing a regular stir among the bigwigs, he was. And he backed up his saying with his healing. Pretty wild stuff. I figured it would be good for business. Crowds usually are, but only to a point. Too many and no one notices any infirmity. I figured this one would draw some interest, but nothing like the mob that came down the street with him.

I stood right up. "May he inherit a barren, flea-infested camel." He'd ruined my morning. I'd get nothing done in the way of begging. But at least I could find out what all the fuss was about. So, I went with the crowd.

He led the mob into the synagogue. They quieted down once inside. It was nothing special. Only a bit bigger than a normal house. But there was no stable to take up room, so the men could gather to pray and argue about the law. We even had our own Torah. It was a source of pride for the town.

He went down front to a seat that they saved for him. He sat and became silent. I stood with my back to the wall near the door. I always stay close to the door. Never know when you might need to get out fast. We all stood there watching him pray. When he looked up, he looked all around the crowd. Near him was someone I knew very well. He had a similar condition to mine. It had come on him after he was grown and already a shepherd. He made do. His family helped. He gave cripples a bad name.

The healer motioned him closer. Everyone, well almost everyone, moved or spoke or stretched to look. They knew what he was about to do. They knew what would happen. And then some grumbled louder. You could hear stray words ". . . heal . . . Sabbath . . . law . . . blasphemy . . ." This was no accident. He was doing this in the synagogue, on the Sabbath, deliberately.

He took the shepherd's hand and he looked at all of us. His words were simple and direct. What was better, to keep the law or heal? His voice silenced everyone. We were caught. Everyone in that room depended on the rules. They gave us control and sense to our lives and order to our days. We never considered anything else. To go against them was to risk, to leave the safety of the unspoken agreements that kept us in our places, safe and dependable. There were no other possibilities. There were no other options. Yet here, standing here before us was something new, something beyond the rules. And we all knew, none had any doubt that he could do this. He could change that man's life, take away his nightmares and his limitations with a word.

The room closed in on me. I felt crushed. I knew what was coming and I ran for the door. I made it outside and vomited against the wall of the synagogue. As I retched, I could hear the murmur grow to a river of voices, as his words became flesh and bone and sinew.

I must have fainted there. I dreamt. I dreamt of that shiny thing in the dark between the stones. Never reach. That was the rule. Never reach. I had learned my first rule as a child, in pain, and remembered it in nightmares. Never reach. Yet in my dream, there outside that synagogue, I reached. I reached into the darkness toward the shiny thing. Yet it was no bauble or piece of quartz. I knew that it was all the dreams of freedom I had ever had. It was a life of my own, without pity or guilt or manipulation. It was a life beyond the denials and the limits I had constructed to be safe, safe from the grinding weight of mistakes and foolishness. Freedom . . .

When I woke, I was alone. No one had paid any special attention to a beggar. I sat there in the shadow of that wall and wondered, argued with myself. Could it be possible? Would the healer consider me, a beggar, worthy? But what would I do for a living? Who would I be? How would people look at me, healed? Wouldn't they remember me sitting by the road? I could move, go to a new town. But what would I do? How would people there receive me, a stranger?

Finally, dusk came and I went home. I hadn't made a penny. The argument went on throughout the night and into the next day. It has been a week. I can think of nothing else. Last night I had the dream again. Reaching, reaching . . .

I decided I would follow him. I can beg where he is. I will decide about the healing when I find him. So it is I am on the road, the road to the healer. Have you heard of him? No, I have enough for the journey. But thank you anyway. Excuse me, I'm not laughing at you. It's just that I've never turned down money in my life. It's one of my rules.

*At once his fame began to spread throughout the surrounding region of Galilee. As soon as they left the synagogue, they entered the house of Simon and Andrew, with James and John. Now Simon's mother-in-law was in bed with a fever, and they told him about her at once. He came and took her by the hand and lifted her up. Then the fever left her, and she began to serve them.*

—Mark 1:28–33

# Mother-in-Law

*I* would never say anything against Simon. He's always been good to my Naomi. But sometimes, well, it worries me the way he jumps into things. He's a big man, you know. And he's got all that hair, curling up all around his face and over his head. Even when he was a boy, he seemed big. Coming into a room like a bull. Even standing still he seemed to be popping out of his seams. And his hands . . . He's a fisherman, or *was* a fisherman . . . How can he go following this preacher? What about his family?

Now I have to calm down. I know that won't do anybody any good. Naomi always thought he was the beginning and the end. And she still does. Far be it from me to be one of those mothers who interfere. I just want the best for my daughter.

Marriage is good. The Lord of us all knows I had a good marriage. Eli was a steady and a decent man. He never beat me, and he talked to me like I was something that mattered, even though I gave him no sons. We had three beautiful daughters and he treated them like queens. Spoiled them sometimes, but never considered them a disappointment, at least so anyone would know. I think that's why they've always been a bit headstrong for their own good. I think it's dangerous if women don't know their place. That's probably why Naomi set her mind to him the way she did, Simon I mean. Even as a child she knew what she wanted. It was a good match, so . . . She never has been one to keep her head bent. She has a pride in her that borders on . . . I won't say it, because I know she's a good girl. When Eli died—"the Lord gives and the Lord takes, blessed be . . ." there was no question. Simon came and put that big arm around me and pointed out the door. I could almost see what he said.

"It's time now, Mother." He always calls me that. "It's time now, Mother. 'To everything there's a season.' Now's the season of your grief. Come and live with us and begin to leave this season behind."

He talks real well for a fisherman. Sometimes he smells, but he talks real well.

So I did go and live with them. And it was good. Peaceful, most of the time, even with Simon and his brother, one bigger than the other.

Once in a while he would come blowing into the house like the wind that drove his boat. He'd pick Naomi up and swing her around. Eli never did that. And I never let Simon do it to me. I thought he might try. I could see the look in his eyes. He's a large child. A good man, but he has the passion of a young one. I've seen him angry a few times. He never hurt anyone, but he can't abide bullies. It's surprising his hair doesn't singe.

I thought it was the passion that took him after the preacher. For a time he came home talking about him. He'd heard of him and then went to hear him with his own ears. I told him to take everything and listen to it twice before believing it. Prophets are as common as lice and make you itch just as badly. But the way Simon talked there was no horror or craziness to hear, except for the healings. Who could believe that? Someone lays his hands on a sick person and they get well. It sounded strange to me. But what bothered me the most was the way Simon took on, talking and making motions and looking at us with those eyes of his. I never know whether to laugh at him or feel worried about him.

And then one day he came bursting into the house, a flood of words and excitement. "He's called me. Me! He chose me." On and on about the preacher calling to him. I don't know . . . Simon's a grown man. Why should he take on about someone calling to him. Naomi, poor thing, didn't quite know what to say. She didn't understand. She was worried about her husband. And here he was walking around the house mumbling one minute, talking to the floor in front of his feet and the next holding her hands and crying about becoming a fisher of men. Honestly, I think men do need a hook sometimes. All they're good for is making messes and . . . Anyway, I stood there watching this whole scene . . . She, so concerned. Him so . . . So I just blurted out. "Well, bring him to dinner. Even prophets have to eat, sometimes."

At first I thought I'd hurt his senses. He stared at me like I was something that didn't belong in the house. Then he was Simon again, and a big smile, his I've-got-to-watch-what-he's-going-to-do smile. I was afraid he was going to lift me up. Naomi thanked me later. I told her to hush up. I told her to remember that when she was tired of having an old woman around.

So the preacher came. And we saw and heard why Simon was so drawn and held to him. But I don't know. He seemed too much of a man to be very holy to me. And he ate and laughed and I even heard him burp a few times. Now what kind of a prophet burps? A nice man, warm and funny. He was respectful to us, Naomi and me. And he ate everything we gave him. And said thank you. But he seemed tired sometimes. Somewhere below the words and the strength that drew our Simon and all the others there was a weariness, or a quietness that . . . He seemed so alone. Anyway, he was no trouble.

But the crowds that followed him. Such a mess they made. He came a few times. We told him to. We had plenty of fish. But the more he came, the more the people crowded around him. And I began to see how Simon protected him and tried to help him. I began to see our Simon drifting away from fishing and his home and more toward . . . Toward what? What was going to come of all of this? If any more people came, they'd knock the walls down. But if he left, the preacher I mean, then what would Simon do?

I wasn't sleeping well, worried about all of this, and what with cleaning up after the crowds, I guess I overdid it. I woke up with a fever. It comes and grabs hold of you when you're not strong enough to fight it off. My mother told me she thought fevers were from the inside, not from some bad spirit. But my mother had a lot of strange ideas. That day I called to her. I remember seeing her there, in the house, beside Naomi. I kept telling Naomi to get her, my mother I mean . . . This sounds confusing. Well, I'm afraid it was for me, too. Mother dead these eighteen years and I couldn't tell the difference between a spirit and my living daughter. I saw Simon, too. I yelled at him to stop trying to spin me around. I don't think he did, but I blamed him for feeling the way I did. Then the preacher was there.

He was standing next to my mother. And I just knew the way she looked at him, she approved. I wanted to tell her what I was afraid of about him. But he spoke to me . . . I wish I could remember what he said, You'd think I would. But all I remember is the way he spoke to me and reached into my fever. . . . Anyway, I was better. Whether it was from the inside or from some bad spirit, he knew what to do about it. I had no doubt he'd done it. He stood there, still the man I'd fed, in our house, the man who burped like other men. Everything was the same as it had been. Except I was well. I didn't quite know what to do.

Everyone stood there looking at me like some prize hen who'd just laid a striped egg. I told them to stop looking at me and go pay attention to him. And I did what I always do when I don't know what to do. I fixed a meal and served it to them, whether they gawked at me or not.

Naomi, poor child, stood there crying like her world had cracked. I hugged her once and told her to go get the fire going hot in the oven outside. We had a lot of mouths to feed. No sense standing around blubbering.

After they ate and talked and he healed a few more, he drifted toward the door. I moved to him and looked at his face.

"It's time for you to be going, sir. I can tell. I think our Simon will be going with you. I understand. It's how he is. He will be a big help. But I want you to remember, he's passionate, he's strong, but he's just a man. Don't hurt him. The world will do that for you. And if there's anything left, send him back to us.

He stood there looking at me with a small smile on his face. I could see why my mother liked him. He thanked me. "I know he's just a man. His passion and faith will be my rock. But I know he's just a man. It's why we all love him. And I'm afraid this isn't going to be easy. Your strength will be needed." Sad . . . As if in spite of all the miracles and glory and goodness there was still so much pain. And then he walked out across the fields, away from the crowds. No one noticed him going, and I didn't tell anyone until much later when Simon began to worry. Everyone has a right to some time for themselves. Even preachers. They found him soon enough, poor man.

They're all gone. And we're here waiting. I think we won't see him again, the preacher, I mean. And Simon, Simon's heart is with him. When he came back from wherever it was they'd been for a few days, he put his arm around me and gave me his look. He told me the preacher sent his best to Simon's wise mother-in-law. Wise enough to know what to fight and what to let go of. There will be more hurting, more tears before this is done, for us and for the preacher. It's not easy to be in the middle of a miracle. But there's no sense blubbering. There's work to do.

*Soon afterwards he went to a town called Nain, and his disci-*
*ples and a large crowd went with him. As he approached the*
*gate of the town, a man who had died was being carried out. He*
*was his mother's only son, and she was a widow; and with her*
*was a large crowd from the town. When the Lord saw her, he*
*had compassion for her and said to her, "Do not weep." Then he*
*came forward and touched the bier, and the bearers stood still.*
*And he said, "Young man, I say to you, rise!" The dead man sat*
*up and began to speak, and Jesus gave him to his mother.*

—Luke 7:11–17

# Mourner

*I*t's disgusting. It's absolutely disgusting. How could
anyone consider this to be anything else? Can you imagine, ruining a perfectly good funeral? Well, it wasn't the
best of funerals. There were all kinds of things that were
and weren't done, that kept it from being a really good
funeral. But can you imagine? No matter what kind of
funeral it was—how could someone disturb this most
important moment in a person's life? And humiliate every
person who had come to mourn?

This younger generation has no sense of what is wrong
and right. These idiots think that just because something
*wonderful* happens, then everything is fine. I may not know
much, but I know what is right and wrong. I know that
there is no way anyone is going to ruin my funeral. I have
given my daughters-in-law very clear instructions about
mourners and food and the tearing of garments. I want
everything just so. But knowing them, they're likely to get
everything backwards. You'd think that my sons could have
found better matches for themselves. We tried. Or should I
say *I* tried. My sons are just like my husband was. Idiots.
I told him for years that Nain was not much of anything.

I told him he should have more ambition. After all, he was a tinsmith. We could have gone to some important place and been something to respect. But no, he wanted to stay close to his family. They were just as lazy and useless as he was. It was that side of the family that influenced those two I call sons. No one can blame them on me. And their wives! They think that because they can keep a house, and take care of children, and be nice to each other, everything's *wonderful.* How can everything be wonderful when I have to be constantly on guard against them doing or saying something that is totally out of line? My work is never done, and probably won't be by the time they wrap me up and bury me. But you can be assured that if the funeral isn't everything a funeral is supposed to be, it wasn't my fault.

That preacher—whatever his name is—was the one who interrupted the whole thing. Not that everything was up to snuff before he destroyed it. That widow had a real opportunity to demonstrate her grief. After all, she was without a husband and now her only son had died. With no man to take care of her—well, let's just say her prospects weren't exactly bright. I remember the funeral of her husband. That had some dignity. But she paid too much attention to the brat. I could tell then, she didn't know what she was doing. She insisted on holding his hand, in public. And she was silent. She cried. Oh yes, the tears were there. But she walked along behind the body with her head up.

You'd have thought she'd put on a bit of a demonstration. I mean she wasn't an old woman and she wasn't ugly. She should have let some of the men know she could wail. It might have attracted some attention of the right kind, if you know what I mean. But no. All she could do was walk along with the tears running silently down her cheeks. It kind of took the fun out of our mourning. I do have a wonderful downtrodden shuffle. With her acting like that it was hard to demonstrate any proper mourning. And now these few years later her son was being carried to rest beside his father. She did the same thing. It was enough to destroy the proper mood.

Then just outside the gate the preacher was there. He stood near her and she looked at him. I'm telling you these religious zealots are enough to ruin anything. It's as if they were in touch with something we couldn't hear. That's very rude, you know. I heard him tell her not to weep. Can you believe that? Of all the unbelievably idiotic things to tell a widow whose son has died. This man was clearly unhinged. So many of these preachers, are, you know. Then he—the preacher, that is—went right over to the bier and, can you believe it, touched—that's right, *touched*—the dead boy. Unclean and ridiculous and improper and disgusting. The whole thing went from bad to worse. The boy sat up and began to speak, and the crowd went out of control, and my daughters-in-law began crying and laughing and shouting all at the same time. Absolutely no dignity.

I got them back in control. I have my method. You pinch the flesh on the side of the upper arm, hard, and then turn. It does it every time. Try it. They stopped jumping and paid attention to me, let me tell you. "How dare you act like some idiotic pagans? This is a funeral." Can you believe they started to laugh at me? Laugh! They stood there and giggled. Then Leah, the older one, said, "But Mother, this isn't a funeral anymore.

Can't depend on anybody anymore. Can't even depend on dead people to stay that way. But let me tell you this is no laughing matter. If you can't depend on death, what can you depend on? The whole world is going to the dogs. When a preacher can waltz right into a funeral and destroy it like that, anything can happen, and that's no way to run a world.

Nobody's going to ruin my funeral. Over my dead body. Why, it's absolutely disgusting.

*When he looked up and saw a large crowd coming toward him, Jesus said to Philip, "Where are we to buy bread for these people to eat?" He said this to test him, for he himself knew what he was going to do. Philip answered him, "Six months' wages would not buy enough bread for each of them to get a little." One of his disciples, Andrew, Simon Peter's brother, said to him, "There is a boy here who has five barley loaves and two fish. But what are they among so many people?" Jesus said, "Make the people sit down." Now there was a great deal of grass in the place; so they sat down, about five thousand in all. Then Jesus took the loaves, and when he had given thanks, he distributed them to those who were seated; so also with the fish, as much as they wanted. When they were satisfied, he told his disciples, "Gather up the fragments left over, so that nothing may be lost." So they gathered them up, and from the fragments of the five barley loaves, left by those who had eaten, they filled twelve baskets.*

—Mark 6:34–44

# Boy

*M*y mother told me you shouldn't talk about people behind their back. I don't know if we're behind his back, but . . . anyway, you shouldn't talk about him like that. I know it's not my place to speak to adults like this, but . . . He's a nice man. He doesn't do the things they say. He was nice to me.

Yes, I've seen him. Yes, I talked to him. When? I met him awhile ago. Where? On a hillside, over there. You want me to tell you the whole thing? My mother told me not to bother people. I'm sorry, I have to go . . . Well, if you really want to hear. I guess it's all right.

My mother took me to see him. Everybody was going. They said we might see him heal people. I wanted to know if he healed dogs. Mine was old, and she died. They all laughed. That wasn't very nice. She was a good dog. She was black and white with a pink spot on her nose. Everybody thinks just 'cause I'm not grown up and just 'cause she was a dog the whole thing's not important. I think she was more important . . .

I *am* telling the story. I'm sorry. My mother says I have a temper.

So we went with everybody. My mother packed a lunch. She always says you never know when you're going to get held up and need to eat. Besides, we had to walk a long way. I was tired when we got there. I had to carry the lunch. It wasn't really a "there." There was nothing there but rocks and grass and stuff. And people. I didn't know there were that many people in the whole world. They were all over the place. They were wandering around and talking and there were a lot of sick people. It was sort of sad. You know, I don't see how anybody could take care of all those people. They all wanted something. Like when there's a market. Everybody comes wanting to buy or sell or get or get rid of. But at this market, well, it wasn't a market, but you know, like a market, everybody was there to get, and all from him. It was weird.

And then the whole bunch began to sit down. I don't know where it started, but everybody just started to sit down. I turned around to see where my mother was going to sit and she wasn't there. I turned around about five times. I didn't get scared at all. I'm almost nine. Besides, I had the lunch. Since everybody was sitting down, I could see better. So I walked around looking for her and looking at the people.

I heard him talking then. He had a big voice. I don't mean big like the blacksmith. He sings while he hammers. You can hear him all over the village. And when you're close to him he still talks with that same voice. My mother says it blows your ears off. It wasn't like the blacksmith's voice. Everybody got real quiet, all those people were so quiet, I guess because they wanted to hear. And you could hear him. He talked about God. But it was easy to understand. He called God "Daddy." I liked that. That's what I call my father. I work with him. He's the best carpenter in the village. Everybody says that. That's what *he* was before he started walking around talking to people. You know, the man we're talking about. My mother says, if you don't pay attention you'll miss something.

So, I walked down toward him. That way I could hear him better. He talked for a while and then he asked everybody to stay where they were and he would ". . . come among you."

I remember he said that: ". . . come among you." It didn't sound like that when he said it. When he said it, it sounded like dinner. You know, when you're tired and dirty and get home and you know as soon as you wash and say prayers you get to sit down and eat. It sounded like that.

I was near enough now to see him pretty close. He looked like like . . . well, like . . . a man who works a lot and sees a lot and smiles a lot and moves around a lot. He wasn't too dirty. Dusty, is all. There were some other men with him. They didn't seem glad we were there. I mean the big bunch of people. They were talking to him like I talk to my mother when I don't want to do something and she knows I need to do it and I know I'm going to have to do it but I don't want to do it so I talk to her like they were talking to him. They had stopped him from ". . . coming among you." I could hear them. They were moving their hands and looking worried and telling him to order the crowd to leave and telling him reasons why they knew best. He listened. But I could tell, you know that look that parents get, and you can tell that no matter what you say . . . Well, he had that look and he wasn't going to send anybody anywhere.

That's when I heard them say there was nothing to eat. The lunch. I remembered the lunch. So, I walked up and told one of the worried men that I had some food with me. I had to say it a bunch of times before he would pay attention. Grownups never listen to us. So, when he did hear me, he laughed and I didn't know if I'd done something dumb. But, I'd done it. So, when he took me to the ". . . coming among you" man, I made the best of it. The way he said it, that I had a few loaves and fish, made me think I was almost a joke. But the one we came to see didn't treat me like a joke.

As soon as he saw me, he crouched down and looked me in the eyes. He smiled. He had lines around his eyes like he smiled a lot. When he talked you could see his teeth. He asked me if he could see what I had in the basket. That's what my mother put the lunch in. I nodded. Then I remembered, always answer with words. "Yes, sir." I hope I said sir.

He wasn't rough. The way he opened the basket, the way he talked to me, I liked him. He didn't treat me like most grown-ups treat me. Like I'm not as important, or in the way. When he asked a question he waited for the answer before he said anything.

So then he asked me if he could use my lunch to feed the hungry people. I looked right at him and said, "Yes, that would be fine." I heard my father say that to a person he was buying wood from. "Yes, that would be fine." I felt like this man deserved the best answer I could give him. So, he took it, the lunch I mean, and said a prayer. I don't remember the words but I remember when he said thank you to God, I felt full, happy, warm, like everything would be fine. Then he started handing out the food. I helped. But then I noticed that there was so much of it, it was feeding everybody. There was no way I could have carried that lunch.

That's when I got the idea. I went to him and asked him if I could ask him a question. He squatted down again with that smile and looked right in my eyes. "Of course." And I knew he meant it. So I told him about my dog. And I began to cry when I told him about the pink spot on her nose. And the next thing I knew he was hugging me and I wasn't talking anymore and I was just crying.

After a while he looked at me again and told me that I'd always remember my dog. And I shouldn't let anybody tell me that she or me, I mean I, wasn't important. He told me that God loved my dog and me. And when he said it I knew it was true. That was when my mother found us. And I remembered the lunch. I'd given it away without asking permission. But before I could say a word, he stood up with his hand on my shoulder and told her that her boy's generosity—that's what he called me, her boy—her boy's generosity had fed many hungry souls and bodies. He said I must have gotten that from her and my father. She stood there looking at him and then at me. And then she smiled and I knew everything would be all right.

So, you see? I did see him and talk to him and I know he's a nice man. He's not a strange prophet or a rebel. I mean no disrespect, but you asked. I think I better go home now. I have to work with my father. He's the best carpenter in town, you know.

Come on, Daisy. I called her that because she has a gold spot on her face. She's still a puppy. She'll get a lot bigger. Let's go eat lunch, girl.

*As the sun was setting, all those who had any who were sick
with various kinds of diseases brought them to him; and he laid
his hands on each of them and cured them. Demons also came
out of many, shouting, "You are the Son of God!" But he
rebuked them and would not allow them to speak, because they
knew that he was the Messiah.*

—Luke 4:40–41

# Tortured Soul

*N*OOOOO!!!! Somewhere in the middle. Don't you see?
It can't be. It's broken and the pieces just don't quite fit.
I tried. I did. For a long, long time. I picked one of them
up. It was my favorite piece. It wasn't very big. But it
cried and cried and then it just stared at me. It was like he
forgot that I was part of the same . . . NOOOOOO!!!! It
can't be. Why did it do this to me? Did I swallow it?
There are so many. Sometimes it's a rat with sharp teeth,
gnawing, biting. Then it falls, a night of darkness, pushing away my day. And it laughs and rolls on its back. All
the pain and pressure, all the pieces torn and bleeding.

I couldn't act anymore and so they looked at me. But
they couldn't see it, there and there and in here. Which
was worse: its teeth or their eyes? All those eyes. They
walked around me and looked into places I don't want
them to see. And it laughed at that. So I thought I'd go to
the caves. A lot of us do that. I wanted to be safe in the
center of a place without eyes. Safe from all the eyes that
wanted to open the secrets that no one should open. I
went there to be safe, inside. Safe until I found it waiting
for me. It didn't look the same. It had a face and hands. It
had the hands that tore at me. Why did it do that?

Why couldn't it be nice? I didn't want to be bad or hurt

or yell or laugh or break more pieces. It could have sat over there and I could have sat over here. But it didn't do that. It came here from there, with grunts and moans and hands that were brown and black and red from trying to get out. But why did it want to get out if it came in? And they reached for me. They tore my clothes and left me without any warmth. And I felt the floor, hard and cold and full of points. The hands took my clothes, and other things. They went away and took my clothes. It took its face and its hands away. But the one with claws and teeth was there, still with me in that hard place, laughing. So I hid in that dark.

Dark, so dark. The darkness seeped into me like a stain, like blood or dye that makes things different than they are. I wanted to be . . . different, but not like that. Not part of the darkness. It drove me there. Away from the pain. Into the pain, into the sharp hardness that hurt if you moved or if you stayed still. In that middle there is no center or shape, just trying to get away. And it holds and eats you. And laughs at your weakness and pain and pieces, broken all over the floor of that cave in the darkness full of smells of death and bats and dirt. It laughed and left me there, but not for long. Oh, no. Only long enough for me to think I was alone. Only long enough for me to get a cramp and wonder if eating was another plot to fool me. Only long enough to begin wondering about the light, and then it screamed again. Screamed like some crowd of cruel children who find a wounded animal and surround it while it crouches, frightened and bleeding and knowing there is no hope or rescue. I lay there, knowing that in that ditch there is only fear until their laughter turns to stones and pointed sticks and ends the horror. In the dark there was no hope. But I came here from the light because of the darkness out there. But that wasn't light. It was eyes that pried and tore and told me I belonged with the other broken pieces that had lost their middle, the memory of their shape, before the eyes smashed us and laughed at the wreckage. They bit and rolled on their backs and laughed. There was nowhere and nothing in the cold dark darkness or out in the bright hot darkness.

Another set of hands reached for me within the cold dark, and I tried to run, even though there was a young voice in here that wanted to stay and be safe within those hands. But any hands were wounds, more wounds, open, bleeding hurts that had taken my clothes and other things and left me with memories of the sharp stones on arms and back. Hands were of the enemy, the enemy that lived in me, making me feel everything except at home. But these hands were enough to hold me as I shook. Teeth rattling in my head, I let these hands wrap me in something from beyond the cold dark and bring me out into the bright hot darkness filled with eyes. And back to the place of eyes. Down hills across the space that kept the eyes from breaking into the infection of my emptiness.

"NOOOOOO!"

It screamed from inside my head and heart. Unable to bite me for the first time in my memory, it did not laugh. It screamed in fear. The darkness screamed with my voice and my body shook. But in those moments there was no longer a landscape of broken horror. There was the world— the sky, the sea, the houses, and my brother holding me like a child. And he cried like a child, pleading for me as I saw through the darkness that had fallen like some malignant night so long ago. I saw the dawn of life, in the evening reflections of the marketplace of Capernaum, as my voice and body, still owned by whatever had shackled me to destruction, screamed and convulsed. It recognized its destruction, and could no longer torture my soul. My brother cried. My body wretched. My spirit sang, free, flying to the light. And my hope touched me and shouted, "Be still!"

It seemed a shout. The command of a battle captain has less authority. But he may have whispered. The beast within me whimpered and called him by name "Son of God."

I could not see what the beast saw. But I knew the words were small. Something huge was touching me. They were human words that spilled out of my body's sore and bleeding mouth. He was power shining though all the dark horror, breaking the grip of living death and setting me free. I saw a corner, a bit of what the beast saw before it surrendered to the glory of that power and went to wherever evil goes when it faces goodness. And then I saw a man reaching down to touch this broken, filthy woman, imprisoned no longer, but embraced by her crying brother.

"Go in peace, my child."

And then I held my brother and I cried. And we went home.

*On the way to Jerusalem Jesus was going through the region between Samaria and Galilee. As he entered a village, ten lepers approached him. Keeping their distance, they called out, saying, "Jesus, Master, have mercy on us!" When he saw them, he said to them, "Go and show yourselves to the priests." And as they went, they were made clean. Then one of them, when he saw that he was healed, turned back, praising God with a loud voice. He prostrated himself at Jesus' feet and thanked him. And he was a Samaritan. Then Jesus asked, "Were not ten made clean? But the other nine, where are they? Was none of them found to return and give praise to God except this foreigner?" Then he said to him, "Get up and go on your way; your faith has made you well."*

—Luke 17:11–19

# Healthy Man

*I* am healthy now. What good is anything if you don't have your health? That's something you may not appreciate. It's probably something you take for granted. Not me. I lived without hope. I lived from day to day without any promise or dignity. I was a leper. That was my whole life.

It is hard to describe. The details are easy. I had to wear white. I wore a bell so that healthy, clean people wouldn't bump into me. If they, the clean ones, needed amusement they could use me. They never touched me. But they didn't need to come close to throw things. They always kept distant. They even kept distant when they threw or dropped alms.

What is hard to describe is the losing. I had a family, a job, I was somebody. I lost it all. The leprosy took it. I even lost my nationality. I was no longer a Jew from Judea. I was a leper. That said it all. We lepers are a nation to ourselves. We hung together for whatever safety and comfort we could find. Samaritans, Jews, Arabs, all the past prejudices and pride were lost with the rest of our lives. A group of us was less likely to be attacked. And when we gathered food and begged, we could provide some for the ones more sick than the rest. It wasn't generosity so much as fear. We all knew we would be there one day, too ill to take care of ourselves. We would be too sick to pick the garbage or beg. We would be too sick to get along by ourselves. And then we would die. Why we should fear that I don't know. We had lost everything else. Perhaps that's why. Our miserable lives were all we had.

We had gone out to beg that morning, a group of us. We'd been camping near a stream for a few days. One of us stayed behind. He was weak and blind. We told him we'd be back. He had been a merchant, rich and prosperous. Now he was a weeping wreck. When we returned that evening the shelters we'd set up were burning and there in the ashes was a pile of stones. I wonder how long it took him to die. We piled more stones over him to keep the dogs away. They don't care about our sickness. We moved on.

There were rumors. Even lepers hear rumors. This preacher was a healer. He was a worker of miracles. As we stumbled on, we heard he was on the road, teaching and healing as he traveled. We hadn't spoken about it, perhaps we were afraid to hope or look forward to anything. But when we saw him and his group coming we started yelling. We were ignored. They tried to shut us away, to keep our sickness away from the goodness and wisdom, but our desperation, all the years of darkness and loss, pushed us on. "Have mercy on us," we beseeched.

He stopped and came toward us. And then we realized he was speaking to us. He stood, close, with no indication that he meant to turn and protect himself with distance. "Go and show yourselves to the priests." In all these years no man had spoken to me with anything but a curse. Somehow he had done something to us. Somehow he had come among us. Somehow he had touched us.

We turned and shuffled away, to do as he said. I will not say that I hoped, but for the first time in so long I had something to do other than lose and die. And as we went, we became clean. We became whole and well. We lost our curse there on the road. We danced and shouted. We ran around like madmen. And then we stripped and buried our white rags and our bells and covered ourselves enough to get to the priests. They gave us clothes and our lives began again. It was hours before we realized one of us had not come to the priests. He was young. He was a Samaritan fool.

But the story is not done. It was months later. I had a job, money, a friend or two, and I attended synagogue. I was a person again. I had my health. The only part left of . . . left of my former condition were the dreams. They chased me though the nights.

I heard that there was a Samaritan madman living among the lepers outside the city near the garbage dump. As they described him I remembered. Toward evening I went and found him. He was one of us, one of the healed. The young fool who never made it to the priests. I came into the camp and my skin crawled to see him there amid the sickness and the suffering. He was stirring a pot. I was terrified.

I was afraid to ask, but I had to. "Why are you here? Has it returned?" He put down the spoon and straightened up. As he walked toward me, I retreated. "Keep your distance." He stood still and smiled sadly. "No don't worry, I am still clean. We were healed." I sighed in relief. "But why are you here?" He smiled again.

"I went back to thank him and he told me my faith had made me well." He stopped as if that explained it all.

"What faith? The preacher made us well. What is this nonsense?"

"I wanted to say thank you. And I realized now I had something to give, something few could or would give. I realized I could help people like us." His gesture included me.

I denied his inclusion. "I am not like these . . . cursed ones. I am whole. I am well. I left this all behind that day I buried the bell."

He stood so still. He looked at me so silently. He looked into me, into the nightmares that still chased me. He was so peaceful. Then, before I knew, he stepped up to me and touched my hand. "I hope you are well. Bless you." And before I could move he turned back to the stirring of the pot.

I stopped running at the gate of the city. I could not sleep that night and the dreams have continued to torment my darkness; dreams of sickness, and losing, and dreams of his silent, sad smile.

I went back to see him again, to beg him to lift whatever curse he'd laid on me and perhaps to ask him about his . . . his peace. The ashes were cold around a few scattered piles of stones. We clean ones always keep our distance. He was a fool. He may still be. How could he risk the only thing that matters. How could he think that those ugly, sick . . . *things* were worth . . . anything? Faith, gratitude, foolishness!

I still have the dreams. They chase me like some plague.

But at least I have my health.

*One of the Pharisees asked Jesus to eat with him, and he went
into the Pharisee's house and took his place at the table. And a
woman in the city, who was a sinner, having learned that he
was eating in the Pharisee's house, brought an alabaster jar of
ointment. She stood behind him at his feet, weeping, and began
to bathe his feet with her tears and to dry them with her hair.
Then she continued kissing his feet and anointing them with the
ointment. Now when the Pharisee who had invited him saw it,
he said to himself, "If this man were a prophet, he would have
known who and what kind of woman this is who is touching
him—that she is a sinner." . . . Then turning toward the woman,
he said to [the Pharisee], "Do you see this woman? I entered
your house; you gave me no water for my feet, but she has
bathed my feet with her tears and dried them with her hair. You
gave me no kiss, but from the time I came in she has not
stopped kissing my feet. You did not anoint my head with oil,
but she has anointed my feet with ointment. Therefore, I tell
you, her sins, which were many, have been forgiven; hence she
has shown great love. But the one to whom little is forgiven,
loves little." . . . And he said to the woman, "Your faith has
saved you; go in peace."*

—Luke 7:36–50

# Person of Value

*I* have no way of telling you what he means to me. It is
like the roots and branches of a great tree. The high reaches
of joy and the low depths of dark sorrow are all part of
what I am. I never would have known them if it weren't for
him. I would not surrender any of them, or sell them, or
put them away because someone told me I ought to, even
though some of the feelings are full of pain. None of this
makes any sense. I'm sorry. Let me begin again.

I used to be expensive. Someone could have me only if
they were able to come up with the money. Even at that

they could only have me for a short time, usually too short for their liking. That is why I was expensive. I always left them wanting more. Please don't be offended. It was my profession. I was raised to it. Now looking back, those roots of my life go down into a deep darkness full of pain. I was hurt and lived in its shadow for years. But now my life reaches out into the world and up toward heaven. I must try to stick to the subject.

It is no secret that to be a prostitute is not a choice any person makes except under the pressure of some need. I had no choice except this life. Sickness took my family, killed my parents and older brother, and left me, a ten-year-old, alone. Only God knows why I was spared. For years I thought he left me to torture me. But soon God became a memory just as my family was a memory. How can God live in a world where nothing is holy? In the world of the prostitute, there is no holiness, only fear. On the whole, I was treated well by the women who took me in. In their own way they were kind to a grieving and lonely child. I had gone to them because they were women who had a home. I knew they made a living. I knew no other women who stood on their own. They were sad and competent. They taught me. There were many strangers in our lives, but rarely were they threatening or violent, at least to me. But every feeling, every choice I made, as soon as I could choose, was based on remaining expensive. There can be little warmth in that. But it was the practical choice.

The woman who kept the house had a gift for making money. She had turned a curse into a profit-making institution. She was not warm, but she had a worldly wisdom. She taught me how to dress and apply makeup, how to stand, and walk, and speak, and be silent to touch, and give, and withhold. She taught me how to take care of myself, how to prevent pregnancy, to keep a low profile so as to not offend the public or the law, to carry a knife, and know how to use it if a customer became brutal. I learned quickly. She said I was gifted in many ways. And she shook her head when she said it.

She also taught me to put aside money. This is not as easy as it sounds. To begin with, we are women, with all the limits women face. But prostitutes have no rights under the law since we live outside of it. So if we are to own anything it must be something valuable enough that others will want it, even if it comes from a whore. And it must be something that is easily portable so that we can move quickly. We can trust no one but ourselves. After all, who would value a prostitute enough to respect her property? I lived in a world of sadness and waste. Passion without meaning is just that—sad and wasteful. But I made up my mind not to waste all of my life.

I took what I earned and bought perfume. I became known as an expert quickly. It is beautiful. Aroma creates a mood as surely as colors or music. The fine stuff is as precious as jewels and less obvious than such baubles. Robbers have been known to overlook a fortune in frankincense and take polished brass. This was my future. When I had enough set aside, I would leave the world of the night and trade in the fragrance of romance and devotion. I knew no security or hope except money saved and wise investments.

I believed in accidents. Or should I say, I feared accidents. My life had to be tightly controlled to keep me expensive. I could not show emotions, at least my honest ones. I could not associate with decent people. Their judgment could kill me. I could not allow attachments. Relationships are expensive. They did not pay. They limited my ability to make money. When all of these tight controls were challenged by some occurrence, this could not be an accident. I can see you do not understand. Let me explain further.

I never had a deep belief in God. God was always a distant being who associated with people who were clean and decent. That I could never be. No matter how much money I made, I was not clean. My life was a crime. So I ignored God. And I hoped God ignored me. But when there was something that overruled all my plans and controls and disinterest, I saw it as an intrusion of something larger than I was. I feared such an accident. If God was a God of random action, I could get squashed by the flick of His toe. If God was a righteous God, His intrusion into my carefully constructed life could ruin or kill me. I expected nothing better or worse. It was how men had treated me most of my life. It was why I carried a knife. But I didn't think a knife would work on God.

This accident was different. Though I acted indifferent, though I kept everything controlled, the very first time I heard the preacher, I felt a surge of something huge moving through him toward me. I have heard that the sea retreats and returns, covering what seemed dry land. So his presence and his words came across my dry life. But why? This was no intrusion of power, no flick of a whim, or even a flow of desire. I felt somehow it had to do with me, but a me that was different than the expensive object to be bought by my clients. Something came into my world, into my life, and touched places and feelings that I had left behind years ago, or thought I had. I knew this man had not noticed me. He spoke to a crowd. Yet there was in his manner a sense that he would not be offended by me or what I did. Somehow he knew us, all of us there. We were not fragrant. We did not sparkle. We were not expensive. Who would pay anything for such a collection of hurt and mistrust? Yet there was something in him that spoke to our souls. Listen to the whore using such words.

If only you could have heard him. You would have known. It was why the lame and the sinners came. They felt their own value there, close to him. They remembered what it was to be a child, even if they had never felt cared for. There they felt it. Near him they knew it. I knew it.

It was the good people who were troubled. Good people are the ones who keep the rules. They live safe lives inside the fences of judgment. As one who has lived outside those fences, and felt the power of that judgment, I would choose another word for them than good. They are victims of a different curse than mine. But the pain they feel and cause is no less brutal than mine. The difference is that they consider themselves worthy. They think they have earned the privilege of judging such as I was. I knew I was not worthy. But hearing him speak of the Father God, I felt valuable. The good people were troubled. If such as I was valuable, how could they judge? How could they maintain the difference between us? They had a hard time accepting their own value unless they could be more valuable than others. And so he was placed outside their careful fences with the rest of us.

But no one could deny his power. As I returned again to listen, I knew something was happening to me. And I was not alone. Many called him a prophet because of that power. Some said that he should be king. So even the good people had to pay attention to him. As they paid attention, they feared him. And as they feared him they sought among their rules reasons to judge him, to blame him for their own fear. As I saw this, I thought I must stay away. To be associated with him would be dangerous. But my careful controls were less powerful than my hunger and thirst for that sense of . . . rightness. Near him the world was right, even I was right. Even I.

So I returned. My business became more and more difficult. I could not accept the waste and the loneliness for money or anything else. I realized my customers were more valuable than they imagined and so was I.

My careful plans quickly became a shambles, for I was expensive no more. And I rejoiced.

I felt an overwhelming sense of gratitude. It intertwined with my joy and took me beyond my careful limits. Somehow I had to thank him. I knew he would be dining at the home of a Pharisee, one of the good ones. He was a celebrity, and so to have him eat at table was a sensation—perhaps a little risky, but what better way to discredit someone than to witness his impropriety at your own table?

I brought the spikenard, my favorite. It was in an alabaster cask, inlaid with ebony. I had no clear plan, except to let him know of his worth, to me. I dressed with all the skill I had. I knew I would be beautiful, really beautiful. I was filled with the beauty of love. I could see it in the faces of those in the house as I entered. No one got in my way. The public was welcomed as a sign of the ruler's generosity. People stood about, talking and eating. Within, the privileged were welcomed, reclining on their couches to eat. I asked no permission. I walked in knowing the wealth of gratitude.

As I entered the room I went to him and saw, of all things, his feet. No one had soothed his feet. This rich and supposedly generous man could not even provide this simple courtesy to him. Perhaps it may seem a small thing, considering what he had done for me, but at that moment, it was something he needed. And it was something I could give him.

There was no other priority. I moved to him, broke the seal on the cask and anointed his feet. But as the salve covered him, I realized I had no cloth to spread and wipe and remove the spikenard and the dirt. There is a saying that a woman's hair can tempt the angels from heaven. That is why betrothed and married women must cover their hair. My hair had been one of my selling points. It was heavy and long. I held it back with pins, gifts from a grateful customer. Gratefully, I removed them and let it fall. I turned my head and took the hair in my hands, using it to wipe the dirt from his feet.

It was then I began to cry.

The feelings were very personal, hard to describe. But I will try. I had taken my hair down for men again and again. I had displayed and used it for their pleasure and my advantage. I had profited from their pleasure. Now, what I did was more profitable for me than all those well-rehearsed acts. In this moment, I gave because he needed and I expected nothing. But in this moment, giving what I had for him, I received *everything*. I cried for all the years of expecting and holding back. I cried for all the years of controlling and using. I cried for the people I had despised. I cried for despising myself. I cried for all the waste. I had never seen it clearly until now. And so I cried.

I realized some were talking. I realized they came and judged me, judged my gratitude from behind their fears. But his voice protected me and blessed me and reminded them, even in their judgment, of my value. I may have offended them, but he was grateful. He was grateful for me. He saw past the years of waste and darkness. He valued me.

It was not long before they arrested him. They tried to make him less by killing him. They are small and hurtful people. That day I wept again. He had wounds no salve or gratitude could soothe. He suffered in ways I do not know, because even in his pain, he valued the ones who caused it. But their best or worst efforts were wasted. He is too valuable to die. And he values us all.

I used to be expensive. Now I am valuable.

*When he entered Capernaum, a centurion came to him, appeal-*
*ing to him and saying, "Lord, my servant is lying at home para-*
*lyzed, in terrible distress." And he said to him, "I will come and*
*cure him." The centurion answered, "Lord, I am not worthy to*
*have you come under my roof; but only speak the word, and my*
*servant will be healed. For I also am a man under authority,*
*with soldiers under me; and I say to one, 'Go,' and he goes, and*
*to another, 'Come,' and he comes, and to my slave, 'Do this,'*
*and the slave does it." When Jesus heard him, he was amazed*
*and said to those who followed him, "Truly I tell you, in no one*
*in Israel have I found such faith. . . ." And to the centurion*
*Jesus said, "Go; let it be done for you according to your faith."*
*And the servant was healed in that hour.*

—Matthew 8:5–13

# Roman Wife

*I* have always had the deepest respect for my husband.
He has provided for me a home built of caring and comfort and peace. And though he is a soldier, here in this
dusty province we have a good life. I thank the gods that
he is not part of a legion that does battle at the frontier
with barbarians. Rome expands its power with the sweat
and steel and blood of its soldiers. And he is an officer
who could not stand back if his men were in a fight. He
has no love of pain or death, but he has great love for his
troopers. They are his children.

They are the only children he has. That is the ache in
the heart of our marriage. We are without that basic blessing. I have been to all the physicians and diviners. I care
not the cost. To give him the joy of a child would be the
greatest blessing I could imagine. But there is no help
there. The quacks and charlatans have just the right
potion or incantation for a price. They offer expensive

hope and possibility. The authentic ones look at me with sad eyes that say more than any words could.

It has always felt like a sickness deep in me to watch other women carry and play with their children. And when I look at him, my husband, that sickness becomes a wound.

Please understand, he has never once said anything that would make me feel that my barrenness mattered. Of course, he is no holy man. He is a soldier. He has been drunk and angry and like any man enjoys himself when . . . Let us say he is a man. But he cares about me. He commands a hundred rough soldiers, but he speaks to me with respect and concern. He has killed men with his bare hands, but he touches me with gentleness and appreciation.

No, it is not he that creates this wound. It is I. There is nowhere to hide from my emptiness. There is no poultice to pull out its poison. But I am Roman. I was taught in the Stoic manner. I was taught to receive difficulty and to set my face against it, like a ship faces a storm. So I make a home for him that is pleasant to come back to after the difficulties of the day, a haven from the cross currents and fights of his life. Besides, we are representatives of the empire. Are we to let natives see us less than strong?

Perhaps it was this effort to maintain my strength that allowed the boy to creep into my being, unnoticed. He was nothing special to look at, a slave of eight or nine years with auburn curly hair as many of the natives have around here. He has always had a ready smile and good sound teeth. But one day this unspecial child was special to me. I do not know when or how it happened. But one day it was so. The world was brighter when he was near. I was proud of his strength and agility. I was worried when he played rough with the other slaves, though of course he was fearless, of which I was proud. It was difficult to stand apart from him. In spite of our distance, my life began to have the center it had lacked.

My husband noticed how I changed and found the root of my happiness soon enough. He, in his wisdom, encouraged me to teach a few of the slave children who showed promise, to read and write. He said it would make them more useful and valuable, but I knew he was seeking a way to support my affection for the child. He also knew that I needed a good excuse to cover my desire to care for the boy. He was a native. He was a slave. It would be less than seemly for me to tumble all over him. But teaching him and a few others gave me an opportunity to have him close, at least a few hours every week. It was a wonderful time. But the boundaries never fell between us. I was master, he slave. I was Roman, he not.

Our lessons were a new experience and he came to learning eagerly. He lingered after the lessons. I think he sensed my feelings, though I was careful to keep everything proper. An affection was building between us that was like a blooming flower in a garden that had never known such color and fragrance.

The sickness made keeping the boundaries more difficult. He ran and climbed and wrestled no more. There were no more lessons. I visited him in the room where the young slaves slept as I always do when one of them is sick, bringing medicines and food. But I came again after a short time and then I stayed. My pretense was useless. Everything in me reached for him, to comfort and heal. But I was helpless. It seemed to be the fever many of the natives get, and sometimes even we Romans. We used all the normal treatments. But after two days his head hurt and he was unable to move. All he could do was cry out, and all I could do was watch and feel a part of me breaking apart and bleeding. The bond between us was obvious. He cried for me. I cried for us both.

My husband came and sat with me, dusty from his latest patrol. I tried to maintain my composure, to be the good wife, to comport myself with dignity, but I cried before him. My duty to him and to Rome was less important or powerful than the need and the pain of this paralyzed slave before me.

He reached out and took my hand.

I still wonder at him. The commander, the worrier, the man of dignity, the Roman, reached out and took my hand.

He bent his head and spoke to me of a native holy man that was in the area. He told me this holy man had a reputation for being able to heal all kinds of sicknesses. He told me he would go and request his aid.

I sat there with the tears of wounded hopes on my face trying to understand how he could bring himself to do this. He owed no man. He stood tall and independent among his peers and far above the natives. For him to go and ask, to open his need to a Jew, was a miracle. It became part of the chaos that tore around me in that room of sickness and loss. He squeezed my hand and left, I could hear his armor clanking.

Each moment was another burden to carry. Each whimper was a desperate grip on life, tenuous and painful, but life nonetheless. I did not want him in pain, but to let him go, to release him from life was too much for me. Not yet . . .

Religion has always been little to me except as social observance. The gods have been little except excuses to gather and be what we are, a community bonded by duty and destiny. The festivals were sometimes delightful and many times a bother. But I will tell you this, as I sat there holding his small limp hand in my own, listening to his weakening cries, watching the life I treasured seep out of him, I began to pray.

There was no destination, no face on the god to whom I lifted my desperation. I knew no god who cared whether I lived or died, let alone would stoop to touch the life of a slave. But my husband's willingness to go beyond all caution and social boundary gave me courage that allowed me to confront an unknown with little but my need.

There was no time. There was only the trap of death, closing. But time passed.

Then I felt something in the room with us. I have no doubt. I know something was there. I felt it like a movement of a breeze through a still afternoon. I felt it in the air and in his hand. I had been holding his hand. Suddenly, he was holding mine.

It was not gradual, like a convalescence. One moment he was sick, paralyzed, dying. The next, he sat up and threw his arms about me. He wept, but I think it was because I wept first. He clung to me, but I know not who clung more tightly. Again time was lost.

Finally I had food brought and he ate. He ate like the growing boy he was. Beyond any hope, he was well. I was terrified. What if the sickness returned? What had been in the room with us? And then my husband came.

He came hot and dusty and in a hurry. But only to get there. Once he sat next to me, he was still. The boy was frightened. He had never spoken to this the master of one hundred worriers and his master as well. My husband covered his small hand with his own.

He told the boy of the one who had healed him. He told him of his power and his willingness to care for a person he had never known or even seen. He told him that in all his days of travel and battle, of seeing so many awful and wonderful things, this was the most amazing. And he told him that he, this young boy, was evidence of a miracle. And he told him that a miracle could not remain a slave. And he told him that we, my husband and I, would adopt him to be our son. And he told him to never forget this day of wonder that had turned sickness and darkness into a family.

And so we were all healed on that day.

*When Jesus arrived, he found that Lazarus had already been in the tomb four days. . . . Many of the Jews had come to Martha and Mary to console them about their brother. When Martha heard that Jesus was coming, she went and met him . . . Jesus said to her, "I am the resurrection and the life. Those who believe in me, even though they die, will live, and everyone who lives and believes in me will never die. Do you believe this?" She said to him, "Yes, Lord, I believe that you are the Messiah, the Son of God . . ." When she had said this, she went back and called her sister Mary . . . The Jews who were with her in the house, consoling her, saw Mary get up quickly and go out. They followed her because they thought that she was going to the tomb to weep there. When Mary came where Jesus was and saw him, she knelt at his feet and said to him, "Lord, if you had been here, my brother would not have died." When Jesus saw her weeping, and the Jews who came with her also weeping, he was greatly disturbed in spirit and deeply moved. He said, "Where have you laid him?" . . . Then Jesus, again greatly disturbed, came to the tomb. It was a cave, and a stone was lying against it. Jesus said, "Take away the stone." Martha, the sister of the dead man, said to him, "Lord, already there is a stench because he has been dead four days." Jesus said to her, "Did I not tell you that if you believed, you would see the glory of God?" So they took away the stone. And Jesus looked upward and said, "Father, I thank you for having heard me . . ." When he had said this, he cried with a loud voice, "Lazarus, come out!" The dead man came out, his hands and feet bound with strips of cloth, and his face wrapped in a cloth. Jesus said to them, "Unbind him, and let him go."*

—John 11:1–46

# Pharisee

*I*f it is not of God it will not last; if it is of God we cannot fight it. That is what the teachers say. But what am I to do with what I have seen? It makes the teachings and

101

wisdom so small. There is no fighting this. I tell you, all my life I have lived within the law and its discipline. You know me, it has been my world, my entire world. I have learned and discussed the great thinkers that reflected upon the law with the gifts of insight and humility. I have found there deep wells of truth that give existence its sense and focus. I have given my life to this. And now . . . what? What shall I say or do? How can I study? I am overturned. My life cannot go on the way it has. But to leave everything . . .? I will tell you.

He was the focus of much discussion, derision most of the time. He acted with little discipline, at least that we could see. He broke the Sabbath. He associated with known sinners, tax collectors, and prostitutes. He spoke of the Lord, His name be praised forever, as a family member. He referred to the prophets as if they pointed to what was happening now. And he exercised power, healing power, that made him famous. But he healed any and all, lepers and mad men and women, and even Romans. There were many of these teachers and preachers wandering around spouting their gibberish, but the reputation of this one from Galilee grew to a point that demanded our attention. What was worse, he did not defer to any authority but the Lord's, His name be praised forever. And when confronted, he often challenged the virtues and motives of any who stood before him, no matter their rank. So the people loved him, as they always love to see authority challenged. And we, we who knew the value of discipline and order, saw him as a threat that grew daily. He judged himself by standing outside the law, the covenant that defined us, that gave birth to us as God's elect and chosen people. But outside or not, people listened to him.

It became clear that we had to act. We had to clarify his guilt and put him away. He was challenging the bedrock of all that was. He was a disease to be cut out and cured so that life could go on.

The news came to Jerusalem that one of his inner circle was sick. This Lazarus lived close to the holy city. The preacher was not there, but perhaps this miracle worker would come and minister to his friend. We would watch and see what we could see. I was sent to be one of the watchers. His own actions would condemn him.

It was at the home of Lazarus that I began to pity these people caught by his teachings. Though misguided, these were devout, good people. The two sisters cared for us and for their sick brother with a tenderness that was a pleasure and a gift. I was angry and frustrated by their entanglement. But I stayed a distance from them, waiting for this teacher. They were not the reason I was there. He was. I did not tell them this; my motives remained hidden.

Was this righteous? I was uneasy with my role because of the innocents. But I thought I was acting for the greater good. I did not see. How could I?

The preacher did not come. Lazarus died. We sat with the family, with his sisters Mary and Martha. We sat with them in this twilight of the end of life. It is a place of pain that wraps the soul in its darkness. The entire house was shadowed. We said the prayers and shared the wisdom that was appropriate. I felt better. This was good. To be reminded of the dependability and presence of the Lord, His name be praised forever, is the purpose and gift of the Law. In the sharing of this wellspring of life I was reminded of my identity and my home. In the reciting of the scriptures and the prayers of grief, I was back on my familiar ground. I was comforted. I was blind.

Then news of the preacher came. He was on his way. Suddenly I was back to looking for the mistakes and malfeasance of others. There was part of me that prayed for him not to come at all. I was the one who was supposed to test him, and I hoped he would not come. I felt the law should not be demeaned, lowered by such conflict and small trouble. But I also knew that its authority must be upheld. So I stayed.

They watched and waited, the two sisters so different, but both waiting for this bringer of trouble to arrive. We laid Lazarus to rest in a small tomb carved into a hillside not far from their house, and still they waited. Between their watching for him, and our watching for evidence, the house felt like a thunderstorm about to happen.

The lightning did not strike until he came. The pressure built even between the sisters. I had heard Martha arguing with Mary. Martha was angry. It was clear she ran the house and was used to giving orders. She was critical of any friend who did not show up in the hour of need. "If he had been here things would have been different," she said. Mary clearly thought differently. Lazarus had been her brother but some-how this preacher was just as, or more, important to her.

"He will come, Martha," she told her sister, "and when he gets here we will know why. He would not let our brother die if he could have prevented it. You know that."

"I know that I buried my brother," replied Martha. "I know that our friend can heal. I have seen him. He will tell me why he did not come because I will demand it."

"Oh Martha . . ."

"Don't 'oh Martha' me."

And so they bickered. And we waited.

Someone I did not know came and spoke to Martha. I saw her go out the door, a storm on her face. I knew he had arrived. My time of examination had come. I was tense and excited.

I followed her into the yard and down the road. By the time I caught up with her she was standing in front of him. I had expected at least loud words, but she was not yelling. I had expected her anger to break out. But she stood there facing him, a calm resolve replacing the anger. I could not hear the words, but they spoke without tears or anguish. As she turned I could see she was puzzled, as if she was considering what he had said. But something had changed in her. The darkness was gone from her face. He had given her something, reminded her of something. What could change a person so? I would soon find out. As she moved, I could see him clearly.

He was dusty from the journey. He had walked. He was not wasted or gaunt as some preachers are. He was of no exceptional size, but as I looked at him standing there, waiting in the road, I realized why so much happened around him. There was a tangible power about him, at least there was then. He stood, hands at his sides, looking down the road toward their house. And though he did not move or clench anything that I could see, he struggled. With what I did not know. I know that sounds strange. But I am telling you as best I can. It was a sense of preparation. That feeling of impending lightning was there around him. As I looked at him the hair on my arms and my neck rose. I shivered. I confess, I was afraid.

Just then I knew I was wrong. Not wrong as if I had made an error in the law, an infraction or a mistake. No, I was wrong in a greater way, a deeper way. A way I had never known until now.

I knew that seeking to trap this man was nothing less than stupid, and against any law that God could give us. It was not his shining virtue or even glowing faith that showed me this. It was raw power. Not power against me or other people, but the power of the seasons, and the storm, and the desert. I knew anything I would say against him would be a lie. Even if he broke a law, he would be right and the law wrong. Yes, I know I speak nonsense. But I am trying to tell the truth. I have learned that the truth sometimes supersedes our sense.

Do not think that this was easy or simple for me! I stood lost.

My mother used to sew garments with the seams raw and visible. Then all of a sudden she would turn them inside out, finished and smooth. Just so, as I looked at him, my world and all that was sure and dependable in it began to turn inside out. I saw that the Law and all I had focused on all of my life was only an introduction to something more. He was something more.

Mary came running. Martha and the rest of the mourners followed. Some of them wailed in respect for Lazarus. But Mary cried as she ran and fell at his feet. Gripping his robe in her fists she said through her tears what we had heard Martha say all along. "If you had been here he would not have died." But the way she said it somehow was a plea and a confession of her faith in him, rather than an accusation. She was speaking of her trust in his power, of her confidence in him. She also spoke of her pain, the pain of a child who does not understand and cries to her parent, the source of all comfort and security. She cried for us all, for all our fear and darkness and confusion. In his presence all our need and vulnerability was obvious.

He did not reach out to her, but stood there looking at her. He raised his head and looked at us. He looked at me, and I knew he understood why I was there. Do not scoff! I am no fool. I have been in the presence of the great and powerful. I have seen and learned much. This was different. He looked at me and I felt small and dirty, my schemes exposed like a festering wound. It was only a moment, but it burned like some fire.

He looked down at her. His voice was almost a whisper. It shook as he struggled to speak. "Where have you laid him?" he asked.

Then I noticed the wailing had stopped. All stood watching. There was something here even the insensitive could feel. Mary slowly stood and, with a gesture that amazed me, took his hand and led him like a child toward the tomb. She understood his was a burden that so exceeded hers, there was no comparing. Tears flowed from him as he walked. I heard some murmur in the crowd that followed. They spoke of him like some piece of gossip. I felt anger toward their stupid, self-centered insensitivity. Couldn't they sense the darkness that he faced? It was the beast of death, and disappointment, and cynicism. It ruled us. It imprisoned us. It was our past and our future. Except for him. He faced its horror, not only for himself, but he confronted the power it took from all of us. He confronted a world of death. Couldn't they feel the searing pain? I was angry and afraid and amazed. In all my life I had never considered this depth. I had never looked past the surface of life. All the time I had thought my traditions and books and disciplines were enough. Now the dark power of death and emptiness stood before me like some drooling beast. And he stood there facing it.

He stood there facing the tomb which was sealed with a large stone. I could hardly breathe. He trembled, or perhaps shook is a better word. The cords stood out on his neck. He lifted a weight we could not see. He pushed out the words, 'Take away the stone." Such was his force that some moved to obey. But Martha came and reminded him that there would be a stench because Lazarus had been dead four days. I think she wanted to try to keep things manageable and reasonable. The look he gave her was full of power that could not be denied. He spoke of the glory of God, His name be praised forever.

They took away the stone.

He opened his hands and put his head back. He prayed—no, he *talked* with the Lord, His name be praised. He conversed with God as I spoke with my father's brother only last week. He is always glad to see me. I can go to him, confused and frustrated, and he helps me find sense and hope. Here we stood, facing death. I felt like screaming, and this preacher, burdened and shaking as he was, spoke of family news, and memories of good times. I had never heard a prayer like that.

The beast still stood there in all its power, its dark mouth open for all to see, but this preacher found something in that conversation, and his burden lifted. His neck relaxed. He stopped shaking. Then he said loudly, "Lazarus, come out."

I had no idea what to expect or believe. I was horrified when I sensed the dead man struggling within the darkness of the tomb, tangled in his grave wrappings. I struggled, tangled up in fear and disbelief. I still struggle. But tangled as he was, Lazarus came out, out into the light, out into life.

There is nothing in the law or wisdom to deal with this. Tell me there is. You can't. It's not there. Do you still want to trap him? To do what? Do you have a cage that will hold him? This man faced death and . . . you have heard.

No, I think you have not. You look at me like an enemy because of what I have seen. . . . What I have seen and what I have heard.

You may stay in the tombs of your tradition. I have discovered there is more, so much more. I must come out. I must leave you, and your dead fears, and justifications. The words he said are clearer to me than any prophet's vision. His words are my new law, covenant, and promise. Condemn me if you will, but I cannot and will not forget them. For just as surely as he spoke of Lazarus, he spoke of me.

"Unbind him and let him go."

*Then they brought [the colt] to Jesus; and after throwing their cloaks on the colt, they set Jesus on it. As he rode along, people kept spreading their cloaks on the road. . . . the whole multitude of the disciples began to praise God joyfully with a loud voice . . . saying, "Blessed is the king who comes in the name of the Lord! . . ." Some of the Pharisees in the crowd said to him, "Teacher, order your disciples to stop." He answered, "I tell you, if these were silent, the stones would shout out." . . . Then he entered the temple and began to drive out those who were selling things there; and he said, "It is written, 'My house shall be a house of prayer'; but you have made it a den of robbers."*

—Luke 19:28–46

# Man of Discipline

*I* am a Roman soldier. That tells almost everything about me. It has been my life since I was a boy with nothing but fuzz on my chin. The muscles and scars and reflexes that are hung on my bones have all been formed by the marching and drilling, the discipline and raw power of the army. I am a foot soldier, trained in the use of the javelin and shield and sword. They are the tools of my trade as surely as a blacksmith uses a hammer and anvil and forge.

I was a farmer's son, born in the sunny country to the south of Mother Rome. My father assumed I would be what he was. I grew and learned and dreamed. I dreamed of more than the pig sty and the plowing. I dreamed of what was beyond. I dreamed of conquest. I remember yelling at him in the doorway of our home. I was an arrogant child. Finally I left, tired of the arguments. I went to the center of the world. I went looking for the army. I puffed myself up as large as I could and listened to them laugh.

They were hard men. I don't mean cruel. They were

hard, like some stone or metal. They were formed in some furnace that melted human flesh and forged Roman soldiers. They wore power like a skin. They were terrifying and I wanted to be exactly like them. Sometimes I see a young boy look at me and I can tell what he is thinking. I have become like they were. But now I realize they were human. We bleed.

Our discipline is our life. We follow our orders and bring the power of Rome wherever we march. Few are willing to even stand before us. They are fools if they try. Our legion's standard is hung with tokens of the best who did try. Except for one. It is his story I tell. Strange, in all the battle and blood, I never faced anything with power like that. And he was one man. Perhaps you will see.

Judea is not a place of ease. The climate is one of extremes, blistering and bone chilling. Armor is a torture device in Judea's sun, and after it sets, the night steals all warmth. There is nothing in the air to hold the heat of the day. But it was the dust that bothered me the most. Any breeze at all raises clouds of the stuff. And to march in it is a nightmare.

The people are the same, full of extremes. They do not take life lightly but live with hard lines. They are willing to contest Rome's power. They will not accept any yoke, even that of Rome. In other words, they are fools. But I respect that kind of fierceness, even though I must meet it with the sword.

I was stationed in Jerusalem, their capital. But capital is not the right word for that city. They have this strange God who gave them that rock. For them it is holy ground. So it is not the seat of their king, or center of their wealth, that they care about. It is their temple, and the promise it remembers. I know little about gods. I join my comrades in the worship of Mithras, but that is part of my legion's code. Gods are less than important to me. I trust my legion. These Hebrews seem to trust nothing except their god. Their homeland and Jerusalem are proofs to them of this god's choice of them as unique and special. I mean no sacrilege when I say that if I was a god and was blessing my people, I would find better proofs of my love. At least I would deal with the dust.

Their celebration of freedom is a time of unrest. They crowd into their city. They remember the defeat of Egypt by their God. Egypt is a good kingdom to defeat. Its riches are famous. But this was no breaking of walls or pillaging of wealth. They won freedom from slavery. Another gift from this strange giver. And so they celebrate and remember and become insulting to us, we who are their new masters. It is our duty to keep the peace for Rome. Passover is not a time of celebration for Roman governors or soldiers.

The news was sketchy, but we had heard that there was a new leader of these fanatics. He was a miracle worker and a speaker of the words of his god. They call such a man a prophet. Miracles and words are not sources of concern, but when people speak of him as an heir to the throne of their great king David, when they gather to celebrate their time of promise and freedom and his name is on all their lips, we must pay attention. Mobs are dangerous creatures. Mobs filled with religious zeal are doubly dangerous. We sharpened our swords and prepared.

The Jewish rulers of the city were no more pleased with this situation than we were. They were realists. They knew that revolution was madness. There would be no winning for them. They had much to lose. So their expectation was less happy than ours. They saw this man as a danger, a rabble-rouser. Such a prophet they did not need. I thought them disgusting. They were neither faithful to their heritage nor honest about their desires for comfort and power. Such folk are dangerous.

So we waited between the dangerous, zealous mob and

the dangerous, hypocritical leaders. We depended on each other and our swords. If they revolted it would be messy, but it would be over quickly.

Our informants told us that the prophet was coming. He was healing the sick and there were rumors of raising the dead. We had a joke that we could provide him with more opportunities to exercise his power.

He arrived on the first day of the week. The mob loved him. The leaders feared and hated him. We watched. He came riding a young donkey, a beast of burden. He came down through the Kidron Valley and up the slopes toward the massive gates. The crowd grew with each step the donkey took, bobbing as it walked. He sat still. The crowd shouted phrases from their holy books and lay clothes on the road. They stripped branches from the trees and waved the palm fronds as they shouted. He sat on the bobbing donkey in the middle of all the noise and energy and watched the city as his mount climbed the hill.

I could see the man, the center of all the attention. I watched him in his stillness and I remembered my mother. I know that sounds strange. But his look reminded me of her as she watched me argue with my father. That same hope and sadness rested on him. He looked toward the city like a worried parent. It was almost painful to see him.

Before he started the final ascent, one of the rulers stepped forward, right out into the road. He shouted something I could not hear. He looked angry. It was clear he was uncomfortable with this whole demonstration. The prophet reined in the donkey and remained still, looking at this powerful man. The crowd tensed, wondering if their hero would back down. It became almost quiet. When he spoke we could all hear. There was control in his voice. It was as if he was telling a drunk that the tavern was closed before he threw him into the street. There was neither joy nor rage. He just looked straight at him and told him that if the crowd didn't yell the very rocks would. He spoke in Hebrew but people all around started translating for each other and yelling it in all their different languages. They laughed. The parade moved on, leaving the ruler standing in the road, an enemy. This preacher would need God on his side if he kept humiliating powerful people.

Our centurion turned toward us and told us to remain calm. We would draw our swords only if we had to. There was no need. A few idiots taunted us, but most were too busy following their leader of the moment. As they passed us and entered the town our officer ordered us to march in close formation and shadow the parade. If they were going to cause trouble, we would be there.

The prophet had a destination, the temple of Herod. Herod is no person to associate with gods. But perhaps he needed to build a temple to make up for a few of his greater sins. Whatever his motive, he built a glorious temple. It shines in the Palestinian light like a jewel. It has been a great source of trouble for us. These stiffnecked Hebrews seem to think their god would be insulted if we placed our eagles on its walls. If their god is so powerful, why are we in charge? The government of Rome sometimes uses diplomacy. We do not seek to cause trouble if it can be avoided. So we have agreed to allow them their own control of the temple grounds. But we observe from the outer court.

As soon as the centurion was sure where the mob was going, he detached a messenger to our headquarters and put us at a run toward the temple. By a few turns we beat the crowd. We went to the gates, but not into the outer courtyard. He was a smart one, our officer. He knew our presence within the walls would incite the crowd to riot. But our presence outside would respect their god and remind them of the presence of Rome's strong arm. We lined the road with our javelins set at our feet and shields at ready. If there was trouble we could respond in a moment.

We could see through the massive gates. We could see the moneychangers' tables where the pilgrims bought holy money with their own, dirty from use in the world. We could see the animal dealers—doves and sheep and goats all raised to be offered to their god—to be bought with the holy money. It was a holy marketplace and a great source of revenue for the empire.

A violent mob sounds like some great beast or a storm on the beach. It is bent on destroying whatever stands in its way. This bunch was different. They called and shouted and even chanted. There was no roar. Perhaps it was the prophet. He came to the temple gates and dismounted. They waited. We waited. He stood a moment and then strode into the outer courtyard.

I could not see where he got the whip of cords that he swung, but suddenly he was rampaging through the marketplace like some madman. I saw him grip the edge of one of the massive tables where the coins were traded and heave until it tipped and fell, coins and scales scattering and rolling everywhere. Then he moved into the animal pens, twirling the whip, as people and animals and cages and straw scattered before him like one of their desert winds. The sounds that rose from the temple, animal and human, were full of panic and fear. Then I heard him, loud and deep above the chaos. He spoke in Hebrew, but there was no mistaking his command. The money changers and animal sellers were routed before him as rebels are routed before the legion.

I heard it said he called them robbers. I heard it said he claimed the temple for his god.

On command we formed to answer a charge of the mob, but they stood gawking. His sudden change from calm to holy rage frightened and confused them. He made no effort to incite them. His actions were not for them. Finally, he stood breathing, calm again. The whip dropped from his hand and he moved with slow steps back through the temple's high gate, past us. There was a moment when we tensed, gripped our shields, as if the power in him would hit us like the charge of an army. We all felt it. The hair on our necks stood up as it does before a lightning strike. But he didn't even glance our way. He walked through the crowd, followed by a few of his disciples. He kept going right out of the city.

There was in that man a power I have never seen or felt, even from the great leaders who order us into battle. Fear does not hurt me anymore. It is like the rain or Judea's dust. It is uncomfortable but I suffer through it. But in those moments I knew another fear, a different fear. Here was something greater than any force I knew, clear and powerful and ready to act in the moment, no matter the cost. And, strangely, I felt there was no limit to what this man could do. Somehow his power was not limited by his reach or his muscles. I felt as a child before him. I think we all did. We stood with our puny armor and weapons and watched him walk away. And we felt, *I* felt, as if greatness had passed me by.

I remembered my boyhood dreams of conquest. I remembered how it felt to want the world and seriously think I could have it. I had learned different. But there, behind my shield, outside that temple gate, I felt it again. I felt the glory of greatness. And I watched it go with a great sadness. My discipline held me in place, but barely. In that moment I knew I saw something larger than even Mother Rome walking there before me. This was something . . . different. I will never forget it.

We were moved to the hills beyond the city that night. I heard later of the arrest and the crucifixion. So pass the enemies of Rome. Time has gone by but he haunts me still: his voice, his calm, his power . . . and one thing more.

As he passed us, I could see his tears.

*Now before the festival of the Passover, Jesus knew that his hour had come to depart from this world and go to the Father. Having loved his own who were in the world, . . . during supper Jesus . . . got up from the table, took off his outer robe, and tied a towel around himself. Then he poured water into a basin and began to wash the disciples' feet and to wipe them with the towel that was tied around him. He came to Simon Peter, who said to him, "Lord, are you going to wash my feet?" Jesus answered, "Unless I wash you, you have no share with me." . . . After he had washed their feet, had put on his robe, and had returned to the table, he said to them . . . "You call me Teacher and Lord—and you are right, for that is what I am. So if I, your Lord and Teacher, have washed your feet, you also ought to wash one another's feet. . . . Very truly, I tell you, servants are not greater than their master, nor are messengers greater than the one who sent them. If you know these things, you are blessed if you do them.*

—John 13:1–17

# Free Man

*I* am a free man. This may not seem special to you. But you have probably been free your entire lives. I have known little of life except being a slave, until recently. I remembered in dreams being brought to the slave dealer by my father. From what I could figure I was four or five, old enough to have financial potential and old enough to live through the separation from my family. My memories are nearly all of people who owned me and used me in one way or another. Some of those are a horror. But I have the horrible masters to thank for my resolve never to be anyone's servant again. I carry marks from some of their displeasure.

You may cringe, hearing of the beatings. But the worst part of the life of a slave is not the physical violence. It is

**119**

the never-ending demand on body and soul. Whatever the master wants, whenever he wants it, is the only priority for a slave. There are no limits or safe places in the life of a slave. There is only the whim of the master. A slave has no right or privilege. A slave has no control or choice. A slave has only obedience.

When I was through my childhood and just becoming a man, I belonged to a family of Romans in Syria. They enjoyed their wine and were frustrated at being stuck in what they considered a backwater of the power of Rome. They took much of their drunken frustration out on me. Most of the marks that remain are hidden by my clothes. The deepest ones are inside of me. In my cell one painful evening, after the beatings, I resolved through clenched teeth to escape or die. Escape is a rarity. It costs body parts or life itself. But I could not go on waiting for a mood to make of me a thing to be beaten or burned. To always wonder how and when the next wound would come, to have no power to persuade or earn anything but abuse, that was not a life I could tolerate.

In my pain I cursed the dim memory of my father, the man who sold me. He had no face in my dreams. But I knew he was my father. He was the one who had brought me to the trader. He had put me in hell. I would escape it, no matter the price. I would never serve anyone again.

I was fortunate. The stars smiled on me. That very evening my drunken master received word that he was called to the heart of the world, Rome itself. He was to be assigned a position of responsibility somewhere in the empire, to rule some colony in the name of the emperor. He and his wife rejoiced. They were climbing the ladder.

As the household overturned, packing and preparing for their trip, I considered my new fate. My first thought was of relief. They were to travel light, leaving their steward to sell off the household and its contents and bring the money after them. Part of the contents was me. My second thought was of pity for the colony that the drunken idiot and his shrew wife would rule. I decided to wait to see where this piece of property would end up before I chose the life of an escaped slave.

My master, the man who saved my life, bought me two days later. After we got to know each other, he told me I had an air of proud intelligence. It was his way to speak to me like that. Kindness was a new normality for me. I waited for the moods to turn ugly. I waited for displeasure to become violent. I waited like a dog used to being kicked. I am able to learn, and I learned again. What a strange new world, a world with kindness as the norm. But even more strange was the respect that lay at the base of the kindness. My master treated me like it mattered what I thought and felt. I mattered. It was not my work or my strength that mattered to him, *I* mattered. That may mean little to you, or seem a jumble of words. Believe me, it was no little thing.

It held me. Instead of planning to escape, I started to learn. He taught me to read and write. He taught me to figure beyond the simple sums I knew. He taught me of the world beyond the walls of his house and city. He gave me life.

I became his steward, trusted to be his agent, to buy and sell and make decisions in his name. I traveled and traded and planned and expanded his interests and fortunes. I became important, initially because of him, but finally in my own right. He even let me have my own money, invest it, and build property all held in his name, but I trusted him. I dared to dream of freedom.

It was a profitable trip to Damascus that kept me away for two months. I returned in the spring to Jerusalem and came to report of my successes and I was shocked. In two months he had become an old man. Something was eating him alive. He sat slumped in a chair, supported by cushions. He should have been in a bed. He waved away my reports and accounts. His voice was low and hoarse. He told me he had a gift for me, my freedom. He told me I was to inherit a good portion of what I had built for him. And then he paused and watched me as he gathered his breath. "My boy, I hope someday you will be free of all the chains that bind you."

I left him deeply troubled. As I lay on my bed, I struggled with unfamiliar feelings. I finally slept and dreamed of the walk to the slave trader. That night for the first time, my father had a face. But it was the face of my master. I awoke confused and troubled. He died the next day. I walked from his house never to return and I wondered about his hope for me. No chains bound me. I served no one. I was a master now, tolerant and fair as I would want any master to be, but a master nonetheless. What chains did he mean?

Two years later, I had my own life. I had my own home. I was a person of property. I went to the temple now as a free man. I bowed to no one.

It was spring again, the season of Passover. The city was jammed with people from everywhere. I had rented one of my properties to the disciples of a preacher I heard in the temple. They needed it to celebrate the Seder. I had no one to celebrate with, I had no family. So I went to check on these tenants. I had heard him speak of a loving God. I did not understand or agree with him, but I doubted he or his followers would cause trouble.

They had come into Jerusalem with acclamation. I'm sure the Romans were worried. But Romans worry about anything that they don't understand. The rulers of the temple were more worried. He spoke with authority and strength that they did not have. I could tell he was a master. But they were powerful. Things were brewing. But

money was money. So I went to check. Perhaps I was
curious as well. This love business, the way he called God
"Father" . . . somehow it disturbed my order of things.

I climbed the steps in the evening air. I heard them
speaking, with a laugh here and there sticking up through
the general noise like a rock in a stream. They were
excited and happy. Whatever the controversy around him,
this preacher was riding high. I came to the door and
stood to the side in the shadows. They had recently
arrived and were arranging themselves in their seats. It
was not luxurious. There were no couches, but the chairs
and the table were substantial.

He stood in their midst. Not the biggest, but full of the
power I had sensed at the temple. He was silent. Then he
took off his cloak and girded up his robe. They stopped
talking one by one to watch him. He came to the table
near the door, took the towel across his arm and lifted the
basin. I felt a shiver in the warm air. I swear he looked out
into the dark and looked into me. . . . Then he knelt before
the closest of his disciples and began to wash the man's
feet.

The room was now silent. He had captured them. They
were aghast. He was their master and he was serving
them as none of them would ever be willing to do. With
every wipe of the towel and every drip of water he
shamed them and washed away their pride like so much
street dirt. This was the duty of a servant, a slave. He was
master. In his serving he was ruining all the careful con-
structions of status and power.

One of them stopped him with a question, "Lord, you
are going to wash my feet?" The answer was calm, "You
don't understand what I am doing, but later you will." The
disciple spoke in pride and almost desperation, "You will
never wash my feet."

The preacher responded, but amid all the murmuring

and all the roaring in my ears, I lost his words. I remembered kneeling and being kicked by my one-time owners. I remembered my master who gave me freedom. I remembered his feet, worn from life, and how it pleased him and me to have me care for him. I saw all at once that no matter how great my power or my wealth I would never be a master until I was loved. He had been my master because he had served me. And so I had given myself to him. As if in an echo I heard the preacher tell them, "Now that I, your Lord and Teacher, have washed your feet, you also should wash one another's."

I sat in the shadows, curled up, face pressed to my hugged knees. The past and its pain washed over me like some receding tide, sucking at all the foundations of my life. One of the preacher's disciples came out the door and paused, looking back. He seemed more troubled than I. He left and I followed him into the street and wandered back to my dark house. It was dark except for the light at the gate and the old slave that kept it. He scrambled up and let me pass. I told him to lock up and get some rest. "Wait. Tell me, old man, am I your master?" I could tell he thought me drunk or insane, and he feared my reaction to whatever he said. "No, never mind. Get something to eat before you retire." I fell into my bed and into sleep.

I dreamed of my master and my days of serving him. I was happy to be with him, even as a slave. I cried as he left me again. But then I dreamed of my father. It was his hand that I saw first. It was cracked and sore and thin. He held my small child's hand so tenderly. And I as a child was afraid, because I couldn't understand why he cried. And I saw his face, my father's face streaked with tears. He kept murmuring, "At least he will eat, at least he will eat . . ." And I yearned to be back again with him, hungry and desperate and at home. And I loved him again, with a child's love rediscovered. And I grieved for his pain and his torment and his loss. And I awoke free. I felt as if I had run all night. But I was somehow free. My master's wish had come true.

I went straight to the kitchen and startled the cook and everyone in earshot by telling him to prepare a Passover feast for all the household and double the food budget for the servants. Then I told my chief steward to go and buy two children at the slave market, "the skinnier the better . . ." Then I ran out the gate. I had to find this preacher. I had some learning to do about serving and mastering.

I found him outside the city gate. I found him stripped for the hardest work there is, dying on a cross. They thought they could master him. They were wrong.

You have heard the stories. Mine is just another. He in his strength did not have to do this. But he did. He served us. He washed us clean. I am His servant now. How may I help you?

So Pilate went out to them and said, "What accusation do you bring against this man?" . . . The Jews replied, "We are not permitted to put anyone to death." . . . Then Pilate . . . summoned Jesus, and asked him, "Are you the King of the Jews?" . . . Jesus answered, "My kingdom is not from this world. . . ." Pilate asked him, "So you are a king?" Jesus answered, "You say that I am a king. . . . Everyone who belongs to the truth listens to my voice." Pilate asked him, "What is truth?"

After he had said this, he went out to the Jews again and told them, "I find no case against him. . . ."

Then Pilate took Jesus and had him flogged. And the soldiers wove a crown of thorns and put it on his head, and they dressed him in a purple robe. They kept . . . striking him on the face. . . . Pilate . . . asked Jesus, "Where are you from?" But Jesus gave him no answer. Pilate therefore said to him, "Do you refuse to speak to me? Do you not know that I have power to release you, and power to crucify you?" Jesus answered him, "You would have no power over me unless it had been given you from above. . . ." From then on Pilate tried to release him, but the Jews cried out . . . "Crucify him!" . . . Then he handed him over to them to be crucified.

—John 18:28–19:16

# Faithful Servant

*M*y master died today.

I loved him. I watched him suffer through the years, serving the damn empire. He did his best. He always did. At least, until the last. But even in the best of times, the skills of statecraft and effective administration were not always enough to make things work. He tried to keep the peace, and encourage trade, and collect the taxes with as little upheaval as possible. He used to tell me that the best way to govern the people was to leave them alone. But sometimes what those people wanted or didn't want pushed or pulled until they forced his hand. Then he showed the fist of Rome. Crazy idiots, thinking they could stand in the way of something that powerful. They would lose and the crosses would go up and the lessons would be taught. Taught but not necessarily learned.

But Roman power and Roman justice care not if you learn. They only care if you obey. If not, they break you like stones in a quarry and bury you to build another road. He administered the power and the justice. He broke the idiots and raised the crosses and moved the empire along. But in the last years he suffered. He was wounded as surely as if some barbarian had stuck him with a poisoned dagger.

And it killed him. Finally he could not face another sleepless night or restless day. I know who wounded him. I remember the man. I remember his seamless robe and his quiet power, power that my master struggled with over those final years. I have heard there are some who say this Jew was a victim. It is true he died. It is true he suffered at it. Crucifixion is designed to cause pain. But he was no victim. He . . . You do not understand.

I must begin again, so that you will understand. You will know why I hate this barbarian.

When my master told his family that we were moving to the province of Judea, his wife wept. It was not known as a garden spot. It lived up to its reputation—hot, dry, and full of madmen. They were so crazy that Rome granted them a special dispensation. They were not required to offer sacrifice on the altar of the emperor. Such tolerance was rare. But with true Roman pragmatism, a pinch of incense once a year was judged not to be worth a revolution. Madmen. They worshiped a single god—*one,* if you can imagine that. And then they acted as if this single god were more important than even their conquerors. You can see why they were considered strange throughout the empire. They might be strange, but they were also considered good citizens, except for their idiosyncrasy. So, the exceptional tolerance.

But now we were going to their homeland, the root of their insanity. It was not mine to question. I had been a soldier. The legions gave me scars and taught me discipline and loyalty. My master had raised me to my position of trust and he depended on me for common and important duties. He was better to me than my own father had been. He talked to me, then. Sometimes I wished he would listen to me. But I was servant and he master. He talked to me about this move. He had hopes. He told jokes about the chosen people we would rule and about their ruler, Herod.

I felt it even then. Like a storm coming, somewhere over the horizon. But I held my tongue. It was not my place. It was only my place to listen and now it is my place to grieve.

Don't get me wrong, it was not all that bad. They were clean. On the whole, they were sensible about most things. Except, of course, for their crazy religion. Now, I don't want you to think I'm a godless man, like the Cynics. Gods have their place. They add something important to the comings and goings of life, a spice to the stew. But these people acted as if their god was vital for every step they took. Laws! They had so many laws given to them by this god. And they followed them! We were forbidden, if you can imagine that, *forbidden* to set foot in their temple! Even the governor, representative of Caesar himself, could not enter the place.

This temple was rather impressive for barbarian work. It was set on a hill in Jerusalem, their holy city. Pilgrims came from all over the world to pass through its gates. They traveled, protected by the peace of Rome, on Roman roads, and cursed us for charging taxes. We should have given them back to Egypt. Someday they will go too far.

They had preachers, prophets they called them, mouth-pieces for their god. Evidently he could not speak for himself. These prophets were crazier than the average Jew. They had no fear for themselves or their nation. They spoke as if they were invulnerable. The people followed them around like the mangy sheep that covered their barren hillsides. With wild eyes, these prophets screamed at us for violating God's law and holding his people in chains. Chains? They needed gags, too. If it had been up to me . . . But my master struggled to be good to these fleas. He told me that perhaps we could bring civilization to them, if we taught it by demonstrating tolerance and justice. And so he struggled. He was a civilized man. He made me proud to be a Roman, then.

We lived on the coast. He traveled to inspect and to show the presence of Rome's authority. That year there was again unrest about all the usual nonsense. Revolutionaries—more like bandits and murderers, if truth be told—kept the pot bubbling. And the newest version of these prophets was drawing crowds. Their celebration of freedom, Passover, was always a lovely time for dancing with their demons. My master went to Jerusalem and I went with him. This mouthpiece of their god came to the city and I went to watch and bring a report. I could pass for one of them, if I needed to. I had learned their ugly language. So, I mingled with them, and listened.

What I heard scared me. He was different. He was frightening. He said hardly anything about us. He made no grand gestures, except to disrupt the animal trade in his own temple. The Jewish rulers hated him. That was clear enough. But they could do nothing. The people loved him. He was in style. I told my master that this one was dangerous. He was too sane to be easily ignored. Though he said nothing directly against Rome, he had the people in his hand. One word and they would rise. So we watched him. I was scared. My master was intrigued. He ignored my fears.

The prophet taught in their temple, mostly about being ready for the coming of their god. I could see some were impatient. Some wanted him to use his power with the people. They said he could work miracles. Some wanted him to start what they could not, a rebellion. If he did that, it would take quite a miracle to save the idiots. The legions were on alert.

But he just spoke about the poor, and told stories, and gave warnings. And I feared him more than anything I had seen in that god-sick wilderness. What he said was so seductive. His voice reached out with that tolerance and justice my master spoke of. But this was a barbarian, and I told my master he should not trust any of them, especially one who listened to voices of gods. My master told me to be still. He did not trust my judgment. Even after all those years. He wanted to know more of what this Jew said.

The prophet was betrayed by one of the impatient ones. The Jewish leaders brought him to us. They wanted him dead so badly it overcame their revulsion of us. He stood there, silent, as if all of this had little to do with him. As I watched him I felt the hair rise on my arms. That had saved my life before at a quiet bend in the road that held an ambush.

The rulers argued and gestured. They made a lot of noise. But there were two people in the room who were real. My master and the prophet. They were both powerful men. They knew. They knew that all else was moot except their decisions. And the barbarian would not even raise his head.

"Leave us."

The command fell like a stone into a small pot. The room stopped, all focused on my master, their commotion shattered by his authority.

*"Leave us."*

The soldiers moved at his repetition and the petitioners jumped. They needed no guidance to find the quickest way out. The prophet was still. Rome's authority rose and walked around him. I knew what was going on. My master's mind was familiar to me.

He was curious. And he was lonely.

This may make no sense to you, but you have never stood before crowds representing the power of an empire. You have never given orders to send soldiers into battle. You have never sent people to the cross. My master had no peers. The other nobility, the movers of the empire, were untrustworthy. So few used anything but their own passions to make decisions. Fear, pride, jealousy, lust, these were their drivers. He had no peers. And in that moment, I realized as I watched, he thought he had no friends. He thought he had no one he could trust.

This one might be a barbarian but there was no hiding it; here was one who was like my master. He knew the loneliness of power. He knew what it meant to be followed. He knew what it was to make decisions based on something other than appetite. They were as aware of each other as lions in a cage.

They talked. Or rather, my master talked. He tried to draw the Jew out of his silence. It was an empty argument. He knew the law of Rome. He knew the power of Rome. He wrestled trying to find a hold with one or the other. Trying to find something that would either give clear reason to condemn or to take a stand against the fear that dithered beyond the doors.

But there was no mistaking the prophet's resolve. Diplomacy had no effect. Frustration is a common emotion for governors. But my master's frustration this day was for something that was impossible. There could be nothing between them except the exercise of Rome's power. Unless . . . And that was the poison on the dagger. Unless this one, this single man, was worth threatening the peace, threatening the local power structure, threatening what it was the governor's job to uphold. Impossible it may have been, but it stood there, quiet and powerful.

Finally, the prophet spoke. He spoke of his kingdom.

"My kingdom is not of this world."

It made no sense. But it was something to focus on.

"So, you are a king?" At least this was the language of power.

"You say I am a king. I came to witness to the truth. Everyone who belongs to the truth listens to me."

Of all things to use on my master. Truth. How many times had this noble Roman told me sadly of orders he had received that made no sense. But even in such conflict he said, "Truth stands at the core of what we are. It is what makes us civilized and separates us from the barbarians."

And now, this . . . I have no name for him. He deserves no title, though there was one on his cross. That was a bad joke, a bitter joke.

He confronted my master, the governor of Rome. He knew the choices that lay before the two of them. He had made his. Now with his hands bound he held out my master's choice to him like a challenge in the ring, calm and full of confidence.

My master had the power in his hand to do what he thought, what he knew, was right. He could stand against these small, idiotic people and their fear. He could be just. He could follow the truth. Or he could keep the peace and kill something that called to him with a power much deeper than political realities. The challenge was there. No one could take that decision from him. Rome's authority meant nothing. It was his and his alone.

And in that moment I knew. My master was lost. He

did not have the strength. He asked a question, and the weariness of all the years that followed were in it.

"What is truth?"

They stood like portraits. They looked at each other. My master exploded. He attacked the doors. They slammed back against the walls and all in the hall beyond jumped and froze. They heard him and his arguments to release this prophet. Rome's power could command attention, but it could not change their minds. They did not care what he thought or believed. They wanted Rome's killing force.

I followed the prophet into his punishment. I watched him flogged. It kills some before they get to the cross. He bled. But when the soldiers mocked him, and slapped him, blindfolded and dressed up, crowned with thorns, I was humiliated. They had no idea. Rome's justice, that's what was being mocked.

When he was brought again to my master, he was a mess. He bled through his robes and from the wounds around his head. His lips were split from the beatings. He was exhausted.

Caesar's governor stood directly in front of this wreck and bent to look into his eyes.

"Don't you realize I have the power to release you, and the power to crucify you?"

He didn't sound powerful. He sounded shrill and desperate.

The prophet raised his head and looked straight at my master. I could see his eyes. They looked past the blood and through the fatigue at the only one who could save him. They looked at him with sadness and, believe it or not, compassion. Who was this man?

"You would have no power over me unless it was given to you from above."

It was as much a benediction as a statement of authority. All the logic and power of Rome was gone, leaving a trap of sad realities. All my master's options had been taken away and he was left with nothing but guilt built on "if only's."

So, the arm of Rome flexed. Only its raw force could clean up this mess. The hammers and the nails and the spears did their part. I followed and waited until they took down what was left from the cross. I wanted to make sure.

My report was of no interest to my master. From that day on there was much that was of little interest to him. It was as if something more than a barbarian had been executed. Washing his hands had accomplished nothing. There was blood still there. It was as if he had handed over a part of himself to be broken and bled.

One day I found him drunk and he raised his hand to hit me. I did not flinch. He was my master. But I realized as he struggled to rise to strike me, there was little left of him. What was left for me to do, to be, except be the object for his blind rage? I kept thinking of the look in that condemned man's eyes.

So it went. I remained with him and watched him fail and fall from favor. I watched him retreat from that day. I watched him die.

So you see? You see why I hate this Jesus? That was his name, Jesus. Why did he have to stand there so silent? Why did he have to be so clear, so powerful, so intriguing to my master? Why did he offer that choice to my master? Why did he have to be the rock that broke my master? How could he pity my master? Why didn't my master trust me?

There is nothing left. Nothing but questions with sad answers. I love one man who is dead and hate another who is beyond vengeance. My world is nothing but ghosts.

*After these things, Joseph of Arimathea, who was a disciple of Jesus, . . . asked Pilate to let him take away the body of Jesus. Pilate gave him permission; so he came and removed his body. . . . They took the body of Jesus and wrapped it with the spices in linen cloths, according to the burial custom of the Jews. . . . Now there was a garden in the place where he was crucified, and in the garden there was a new tomb in which no one had ever been laid. And so . . . they laid Jesus there.*

*Early on the first day of the week, while it was still dark, Mary Magdalene came to the tomb and saw that the stone had been removed from the tomb. . . .*

*But Mary stood weeping outside the tomb. As she wept, she bent over to look into the tomb; and she saw two angels in white, sitting where the body of Jesus had been lying, one at the head and the other at the feet. They said to her, "Woman, why are you weeping?" She said to them, "They have taken away my Lord, and I do not know where they have laid him." When she had said this, she turned around and saw Jesus standing there, but she did not know that it was Jesus. Jesus said to her, "Woman, why are you weeping? Whom are you looking for? Supposing him to be the gardener, she said to him, "Sir, if you have carried him away, tell me where you have laid him, and I will take him away." Jesus said to her, "Mary!" She turned and said to him in Hebrew, "Rabbouni!" (which means Teacher). Jesus said to her, "Do not hold on to me, because I have not ascended to the Father. . . ." Mary Magdalene went and announced to the disciples, "I have seen the Lord."*

—John 19:38–20:18

# Gardener

*T*he cemetery was mine. Or perhaps it had become the other way around, lately. I had put so much of myself into making it a place of lush, blooming beauty that there was more of me in the shrubs and trees and flowers than there was walking around.

She had taught me the power of living things. She had shown me, even as a child, to cherish the life that pulsed up from the ground. She had shared life, been intimate with the green beings that dress, and feed, and adorn the earth. It was because of her that I learned the magic, the natural magic, of creating a place of life—lush life and beauty, where before there had been stones and clay and gravel. It was because of her I was selected by the wealthy owners to create a garden out of the ravine that they had chosen as a place to entomb their families. Her skill, working into the dirt through my hands, had done what my patrons wanted. But all her skill and power and intimacy with life had not changed the simple fact that she was gone beyond any desire or nurture or creative power. My mother was dead.

This whole tale is jumbled and confused. It tangles worse every time I tell it, like the roots of a weed embedded in a stone. It is breaking apart what was. Everything is different.

She had been dead almost a year when Passover came to Jerusalem. I was basically living in the cemetery, dawn to dusk. The work was paying off. Things were blooming and flourishing. My family, my brothers and sisters, came and talked to me at my work.

They went away shaking their heads. I didn't want to hear about the family. I didn't want to hear about my father, or their children. I had work to do. Days ran into days, but I remember that one. It was a Friday, troubled and ugly. A brooding storm had threatened since morning, and an earthquake had shaken loose a boulder I had arranged with others.

I argued with her as I wrestled it back into place. "There is no sense or reason for me to waste my time and make them uncomfortable. They have their lives and have no need of me. Rachael will tell me my hands are dirty and that I don't eat enough. Ruben will make bad jokes about dead rich people. Whatever people may call it, it is just another day. They don't need me for their celebration."

As if in reply the storm broke. A blast of wind tore through the ravine, splitting a tree in two that reached over the slope there. Rain pelted for a moment, stinging like hail driven by the desperate wind. I lost my footing and sat down hard. Perhaps I bumped my head, but I thought I heard a wail of grief or anguish. I had heard those in the garden before, it was a place of death. But this came from no human throat. I sat there, slightly dazed by the horror of it. Then it passed, leaving a dull throb behind my eyes and a mess to clean up.

The light was fading when they came, a strange procession. This is a place of beauty and dignity. The people who have gone to the trouble and expense to create this garden are not ones to rush about without dignity. But this was rushed. I knew Joseph and his family. They were good, kind people. They had come and spoken with me many times, helping create the setting for the tomb. Joseph walked with the small group that brought the body. He pointed the way. When he saw me he came and assured me all was proper. But the tears in his eyes, and the bloodstained grave clothes wrapping the body he accompanied, contradicted his assurance.

It had been such a strange day, and now this procession. Why did they come to Joseph's tomb? I inquired who of his family had died. "No, it is not one of us," Joseph said, "Though I almost wish it were I instead of him." As he spoke, he turned toward the group approaching the tomb. Three men carried the burden. Three women now stood to the side of the dark hole carved into the hillside. They wept and spoke in whispers, touching each other as if such simple affection could heal the ache of death.

The men paused at the tomb's door. It was narrow and low, providing an awkward passage into the darkness. They lowered their voices, embarrassed at their difficulty and loss of what little dignity there was left. It is all that death leaves us when it plunders our lives. It is empty. We are reminded of our weakness, of the uselessness of all our plans, and philosophies, and capabilities. So we wrap ourselves in dignity, a frail garment in a cold wasteland.

"Sir, I do not mean to offer disrespect," I spoke, "but who is this? Is that blood?" It was a question asked in frustration. This went against every bit of order and decorum, but as soon as I said it, I regretted it. What right did I, a gardener, have to question this wealthy and obviously grieving man? But he took no offense. He looked at me with such sadness that I knew this broken body that was being handed through the small door of the tomb was a personal tragedy for him. "He was crucified, humiliated and tortured for all to see," the old man told me. As he spoke, he turned again to the tomb where the women now stood, crowded and stooping, speaking and directing the men who were within.

"Crucified? A criminal? Why do you bring him . . . here?"

Joseph stood and looked at me. "He was no criminal. He was a prophet and they hated what he said and did. Some of us thought he was . . . might have been . . . But now . . ."

So, this was the prophet, the one who'd caused such an uproar. I was there. I had seen the entry. Hosanna, they'd cried. So much for popularity.

"He healed the sick, he gave the hopeless . . . ," Joseph said, "It was the least I could do." He ran down like a runner who has lost his wind.

Two of the women were in the tomb now and the men stood, studying the stone that would seal the doorway. It was braced and wedged to one side. "Eli, would you help? We must seal the tomb. We don't know what they will do to him if we do not protect him."

Like a fool I cried, "Who would defile a poor man's grave?"

"The chief priests and rulers. They not only want to kill him, . . . well, they have killed him. But they also wish to discredit him." Then an idea occurred to him. "Could you watch? Not to guard but to let us know if anything or anybody . . . ?" He seemed at a loss again.

You must understand I have no fear of graveyards, this one especially. The dead are beyond caring. They are as all living things become, food for the soil and that which comes in the next season. But I had no wish to become entangled in this difficulty. These were powerful people of which Joseph spoke. Yet I hesitated as I saw this good man's grief and anguish. He had stepped in and shouldered this responsibility at great cost. He needed someone to help. He deserved it. So I spoke with my heart rather than my head. "Of course, sir," I promised. "I will keep watch for you."

We walked toward the tomb. Everyone stood outside now. The stone, with much pushing and grunting, was edged up a bit on its track so that the wedges could be removed. Released, it rolled down and fell into the slot carved in front of the opening. The sound was hollow and ugly. It shook the ground. No one moved or said anything. We all stood there dumb, staring at a stone. Only soft weeping broke the silence.

I thought it ironic, this man known for his holiness was buried like a thief, without a word of blessing or comfort. But in the end, no matter what words are said, the darkness takes us. It was clear these few who stood before the stone were hurt, and now that the body was in the tomb, they did not know where to go or what to do. I broke the silence, hoping it would get them moving. "So, I will watch and come to you if anything happens." As if I had reminded them to breathe they turned to me.

Joseph spoke, "Yes, good, fine . . ."

I turned away from the tomb and walked, without a destination except to give them an example of movement. They wandered slowly down the path and out of sight. I crossed the ravine I knew so well and sat down on a rock, facing the tomb. I could feel the sun's warmth trapped in it. I remember thinking, "I will have little to report. Even if anyone does care enough to bother a dead man, they will not be able to move that stone."

Later I went to get my cloak and a wineskin I kept in a small shed near the entrance. The trapped warmth in the rock and the wine in the skin would keep me comfortable. I sat down with my back to the rock and considered Joseph's reaction to this prophet's death.

This man wasn't even his family. Joseph was a good man, but a bit on the soft side. Death is death, natural as the sun setting and a flower withering. Grief was a waste of time. I would watch for him, because of his kindness. I could do that. I drank some wine and settled in. I watched the stars and thought of my gardens. In the deepening darkness I slept among the dead.

Though the Sabbath law forbids work of any kind, I work in my gardens. There is always work. I rose in the gray dawn and worked until midday. In the heat I retreated to the city to get food from my house. I was rarely there, except to sleep. I took bread and cheese back to the garden.

In the late afternoon I chewed, and considered the stone, unmoved. If I hadn't known there was a tomb behind it, it would have seemed a part of the earth. The earth had taken the prophet. But there was no comfort in that. I was suddenly angry. There was no good reason for it. I told myself that. But in Saturday's twilight myself did not listen. Death is reasonable, it is part of life; all things die. They wither and die. I reasoned and calmly reported this. And I stared at that ugly stone and hated it.

I was tired of its power. I was tired of death's reason and death's dark silence. I was tired of withering and dying. And I felt powerless. This garden would die when I withered. All my work, gone. Nothing lasted. Nothing. And all we were left with—good, powerful, kind or otherwise—was darkness and silence, sealed behind the ugly stone of death that no one can roll away. I brooded. I drank. I slept. I dreamed. I had not dreamed for a long time. Since she died.

I was small again, dirty as only a small child can get. I had been digging next to a tree. Its roots fascinated me. I came into the house and she met me with a laugh—that soft laugh she had. She knelt in front of me and began washing the dirt away, all the while telling me that there was more to life than death.

It was cool. We were not in the house anymore, but in my garden. "See?" she said, pointing as she did. "You know about life. It is in your hands. It comes from inside you and sings with the earth. I am not far from you. But you must live. You must cultivate your life like the precious garden it is."

I whined like a child. "Shhhh," she said. It was not to silence but to comfort me. "I know you miss me. Let yourself feel your loss and you will discover a greater gift."

"What gift?" I reached toward her and she shone bright and then brighter still.

It was the light that woke me. I was muddled. I thought I was still asleep. I was crying. My mother was gone but there was light beyond brightness. It came from across the ravine. It came around the stone. I couldn't have moved even if I'd thought to.

Then I heard it. It groaned. It was so heavy. I had heard its ugly statement on Friday. Now it groaned as it slid back out of the hole and back away from the tomb entrance. It did not go easily, this locked door of death. It seemed so much more than a stone. But there was a brightness within that darkness, a brightness that would not be denied. And then it fell. It toppled like some con-quered beast and its fall shook the earth I sat on. The light was dazzling. It filled all my vision.

The next I knew it was gray, the gray before dawn. I stood on shaky legs, leaning on a tree, trying to disbelieve my sight. But logic was gone. No matter the arguments, the stone lay there in front of the open tomb. I did not need to look into the hole. I knew the prophet was not there.

I wandered out of my garden. I wandered and I cried. I cried for the tenderness and laughter that I loved. I cried for my loneliness and my pain that I could not bring to her. I cried for the ache of not hearing her voice. I cried at not being able to ask or tell or wonder with her. I cried. And finally I stood in front of my sister's house, exhausted. When I saw her I cried again, but now, we were not alone in our grief, and it became the bond that creates.

There are many stories about that day. I have no argu-ment or logic. I do not know much, but I know this. I am alive. The stone that darkened my life is gone. I am not wealthy or worthy, but I have a garden. And oh, you should see it bloom.